Iron Age sites in central southern England

B W Cunliffe

1976

Research Report 16   The Council for British Archaeology

ISBN 0 900312 32 7

The Council for British Archeology
7 Marylebone Road
London NW1 5HA

Printed in England by The Chameleon Press Limited,
Auckland Works, Abyssinia Road, London SW11 1ER.

Contents

The Pre-Roman Iron Age Hillfort at Torberry, Sussex

THE SITE (Fig.1)

The hill of Great Torberry (pronounced Tarbury) is an out-lier of Lower Chalk extending north from the scarp slope of the Sussex Downs (Pl. 1). It lies 3 miles (5 km) south-east of Petersfield in the Sussex parish of South Harting (grid reference SU 779204). The fort occupies the crest of the hill, which rises to a height of 511 ft OD (156 m), that is about 300 ft (91 m) above the surrounding shelf of Upper Greensand. The hill is elongated in an east–west direction and is joined to the Downs by a neck of chalk known as Little Torberry. Thus the fort is optimally sited to exploit the resource potentials of the chalk Downs, the greensand,

and the Weald. A constant supply of fresh water can at present be obtained within ½ mile (about 1 km) from the site (Fig.1, C).

THE SURVIVING FEATURES (Fig.2)

The defences of the hillfort were constructed around the contour of the hill and for the most part consist of a single ditch backed by a rampart. The hill was extensively ploughed in the late medieval period, during which time the Iron Age earthworks were substantially obscured, much of the southern defence being used as a contemporary field

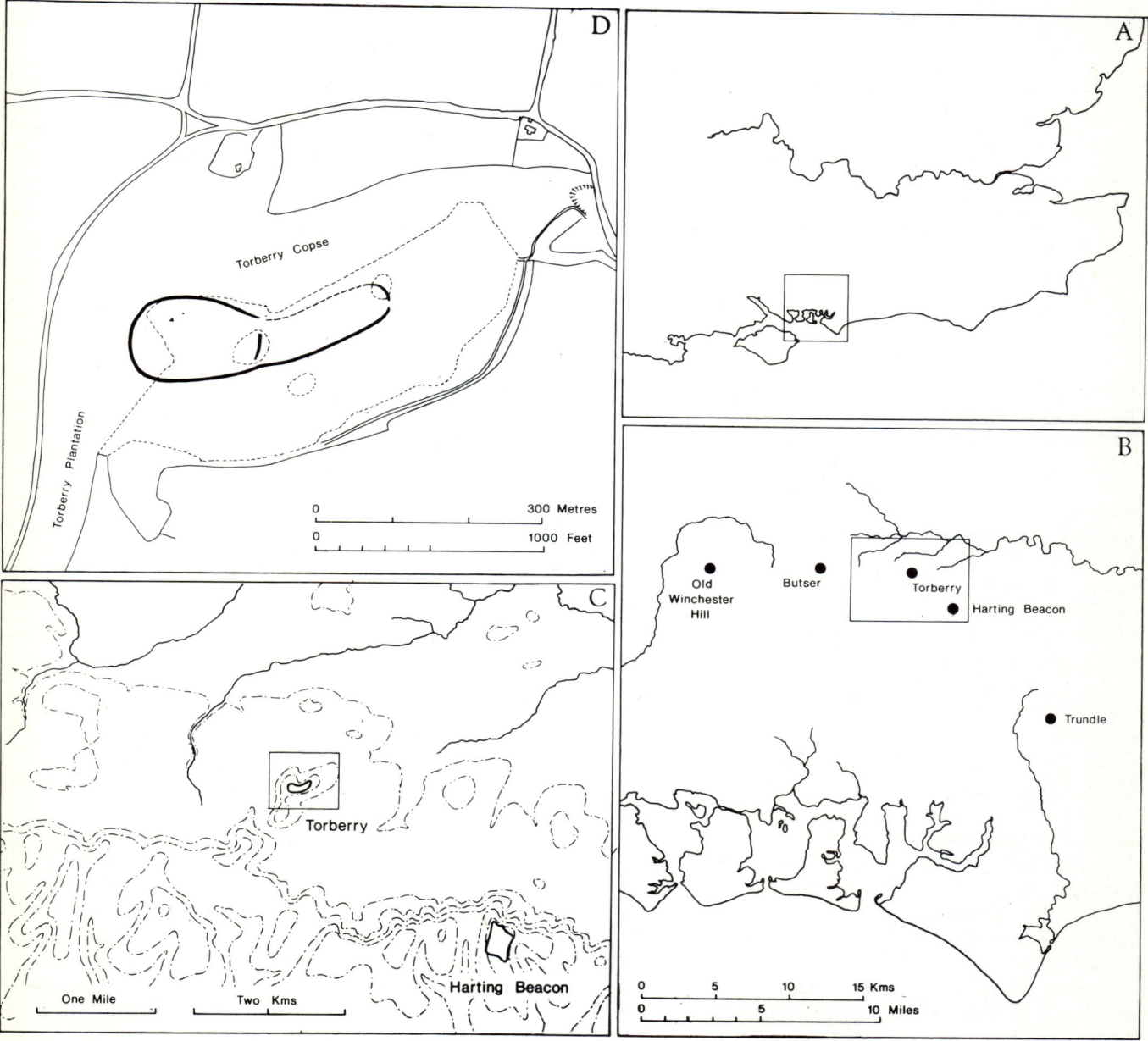

Fig.1   Torberry: Situation plan

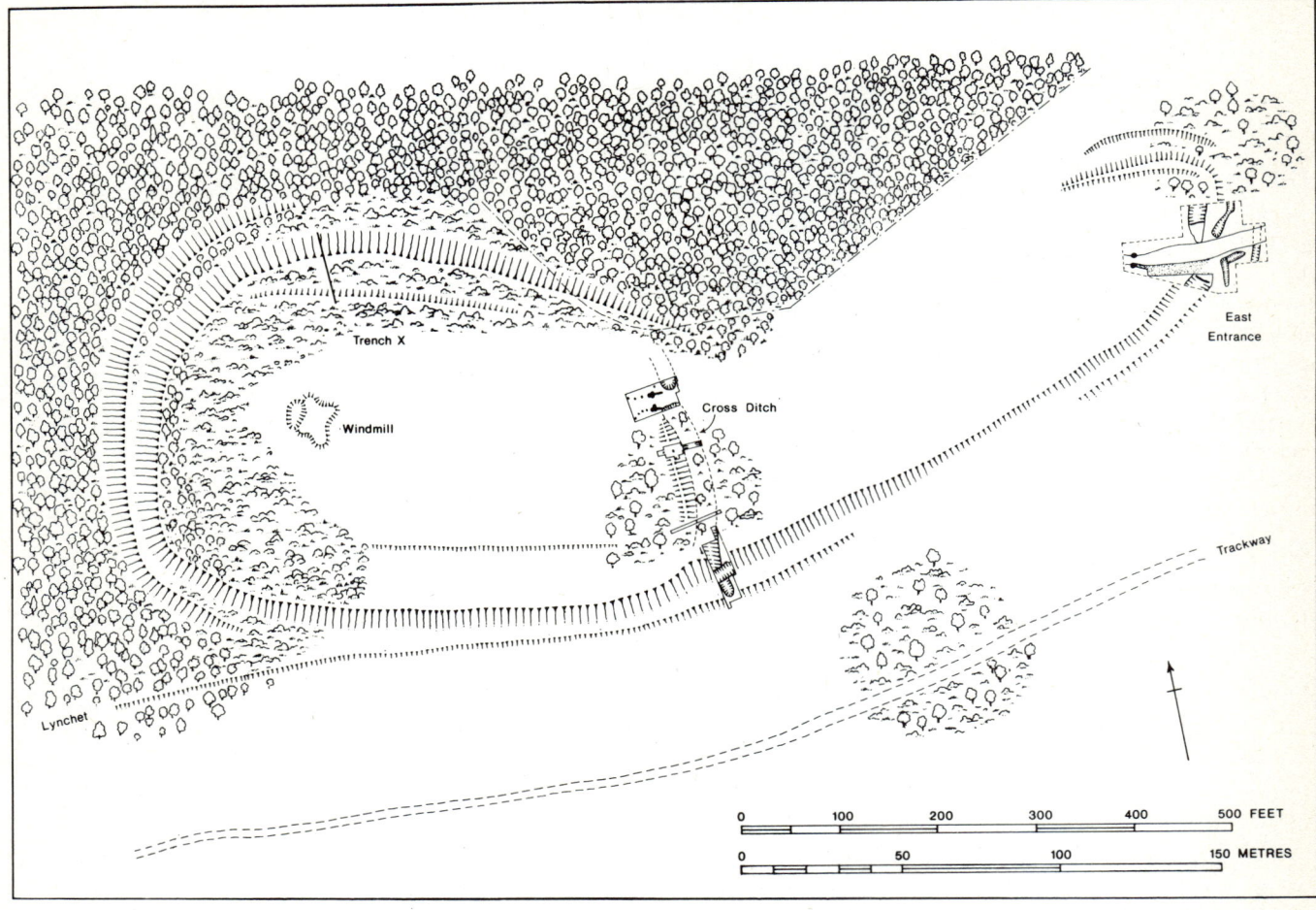

Fig.2   *Torberry: General plan of site showing the positions of the excavations*

boundary. The north-west sector, however, appears to have escaped ploughing and in the woodland which now covers much of the area the rampart still stands to 8 ft (2.4 m) above the silting of the ditch. The centre of the fort, where the ridge is at its narrowest, is occupied by a small copse in which the remains of a cross-bank and ditch still survive, significantly aligned on a change in direction apparent in the southern defensive line. Another copse occupies the eastern end of the enclosure, preserving a further length of earthwork. Immediately to the south of this lay the east entrance (pp. 8–13), but surface features have been totally obliterated by late medieval ploughing.

The hill slopes away steeply on the north, west, and south sides, except for the narrow ridge running from the south-west corner. A terraced trackway, which can be traced along the southern face of the hill, turns south along the ridge towards the Downs. The eastern flank of the hill is more gentle. A hollowed trackway can be made out leading towards the site of the main gate and continuing into the eastern half of the fort. Whatever its origin, it must have been used in the late medieval period, since it is clearly related to the layout of strip fields, traces of which cover the eastern flank of the hill, and may have led to a windmill on the summit, the mound of which still survives.

In the last 30 years, areas of the hill top have been ploughed from time to time, but today the entire hill is permanent downland pasture for sheep. The decline in the rabbit population in recent years has allowed scrub to spread rapidly over much of the north-west part of the hill top, obscuring earthworks which only 18 years ago could be traced with little difficulty. Apart from the continuation of this process, there is likely to be little further change in the near future.

DISCOVERY AND EXCAVATION

The hillfort was discovered in 1948 by the late Horace Brightwell, a local builder and amateur archaeologist. With the assistance of Mr A T Taylor, also of South Harting, he cut eleven trial trenches across the hillfort ditch, thus establishing the complete plan of the enclosure. Two further trial trenches sectioned the cross-ditch and two areas amounting to some 900 ft^2 were excavated immediately to the west of it, exposing several storage pits. A selection of pottery from these excavations is now stored in Barbican House Museum, Lewes, and Mr Brightwell's notes have been placed in the West Sussex County Record Office at Chichester. When, between 1950 and 1952, the hill top was ploughed, Dr E C Curwen visited the site with Mr Brightwell and collected surface potsherds. He records (Curwen 1954, 236) that pottery of the early pre-Roman Iron Age was common in the western part of the site, the eastern part producing only later pre-Roman Iron Age material, the implication being that the cross-ditch marked the limit of the original enclosure, which was later extended to the east.

In the spring of 1956, trial excavation began under the direction of Mr J R Boyden. One trench was cut through

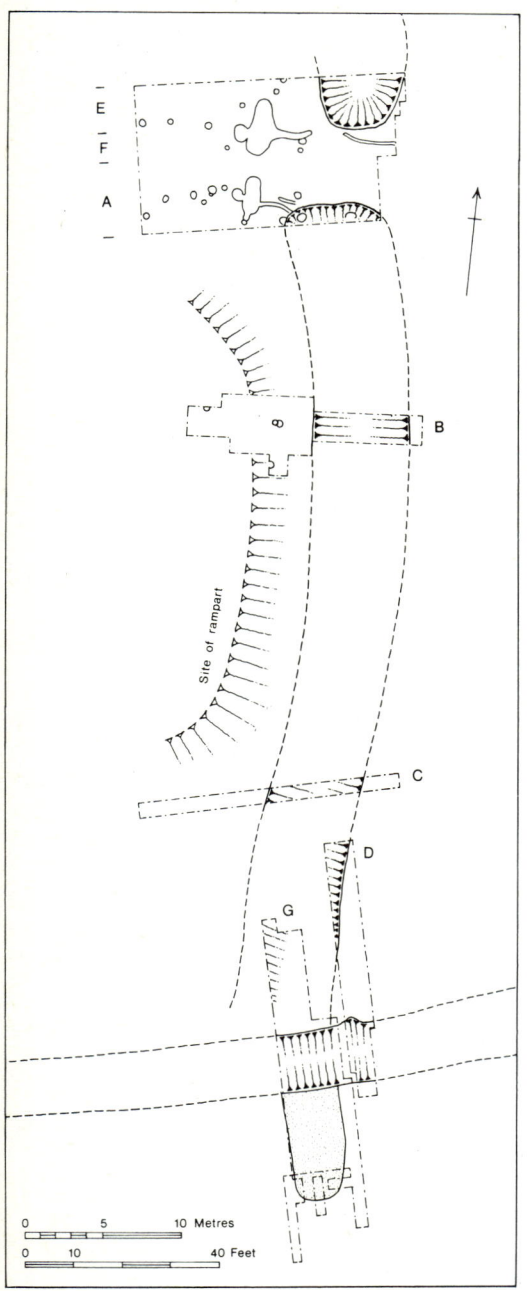

Fig.3 Cross-ditch (site 2)

the defences in the north-western part of the site, another through the east entrance. In the following year, under the auspices of the Joint Archaeological Committee, a two-week excavation was organized to examine the east entrance in detail. The site work was directed by Dr G Duncan, while the project continued to be administered by Mr Boyden. In the summer of 1958, a further two-week season of excavations was undertaken under similar management, the work concentrating on two sites, the east entrance and the cross-defence. The examination of the junction between the cross-defence and the southern defence was completed at weekends in the autumn of 1958.

In the autumn of 1973 Mr Boyden invited the present writer, who served as a supervisor throughout the excavation, to prepare the material for publication.

DESCRIPTION OF THE EXCAVATIONS, 1956–8

The excavations can be divided into three separate parts: a single trial trench cut across the north-western defences in 1956; the examination of the cross-defences in 1958; and the excavation of the east entrance from 1956 to 1958.

In the following section a description of the individual features is offered. A general assessment of the structural development of the site related to the ceramic sequence follows on pp. 25–6.

Trench through the north-western defences: Trench X
(Fig.9, section 5)

A single trench 77 ft 6 in (23.62 m) long by 3 ft (0.91 m) wide, was cut across the line of the bank and ditch. The ditch at this point was approximately 8 ft (2.4 m) wide and 6 ft (1.8 m) deep, with a V-shaped profile. It had silted up naturally to the level at which a thin turf line had formed towards the top. Above this was a thin layer of chalky soil which had presumably resulted from later ploughing (layer 3).

The rampart had almost entirely disappeared except for a spread of chalk blocks (layer 2), surviving to a maximum thickness of 9 in (0.23 m), which had been laid on the original ground surface after the removal of the original turf. One posthole, 9 in (0.23 m) in diameter and 9 in (0.23 m) deep, was found where the front of the rampart is likely to have been. Behind the rampart the natural chalk had been hollowed and trampled by wear over a width of some 16 ft (4.88 m). The slight terrace thus formed can still be traced as a surface feature, but its date is unknown.

Excavations across the cross-defence: Site 2, trenches A–G
(Figs 3–5, 8, 9)

The excavation will be described in three parts:

a. trenches across the line of the cross-bank and ditch: trenches B and C.

b. The area excavation of the original inner entrance: trenches A, E, and F.

c. The junction of the cross-defence and the south side of the fort: trenches D and G.

Trenches across the cross-defence: trenches B and C
(Figs 4, 8)

Trench B exposed a typical section of the rampart and ditch at a point where the rampart was best preserved. The ditch was flat-bottomed, approximately 8 ft (2.4 m) deep and 18–20 ft (5.5–6.0 m) wide. The lower silting (layers 12, 11, and 10) was the result of natural processes, principally the weathering of the ditch sides. Above this, however, the ditch had been packed with large, freshly quarried chalk blocks (layer 9) which are most likely to have been derived from the slighting of the rampart or from the digging of the new ditch at the time when the fort was extended to the east. Above the packing, further lenses of frost-shattered chalk had washed in (layers 5 and 4).

The rampart, of large chalk blocks (layer 13), survived to a height of 2 ft (0.61 m). The blocks had been placed directly on the surface of the natural chalk from which the turf had been stripped. Three postholes were found, one of

3

TRENCHES A, E, F (INNER ENTRANCE)

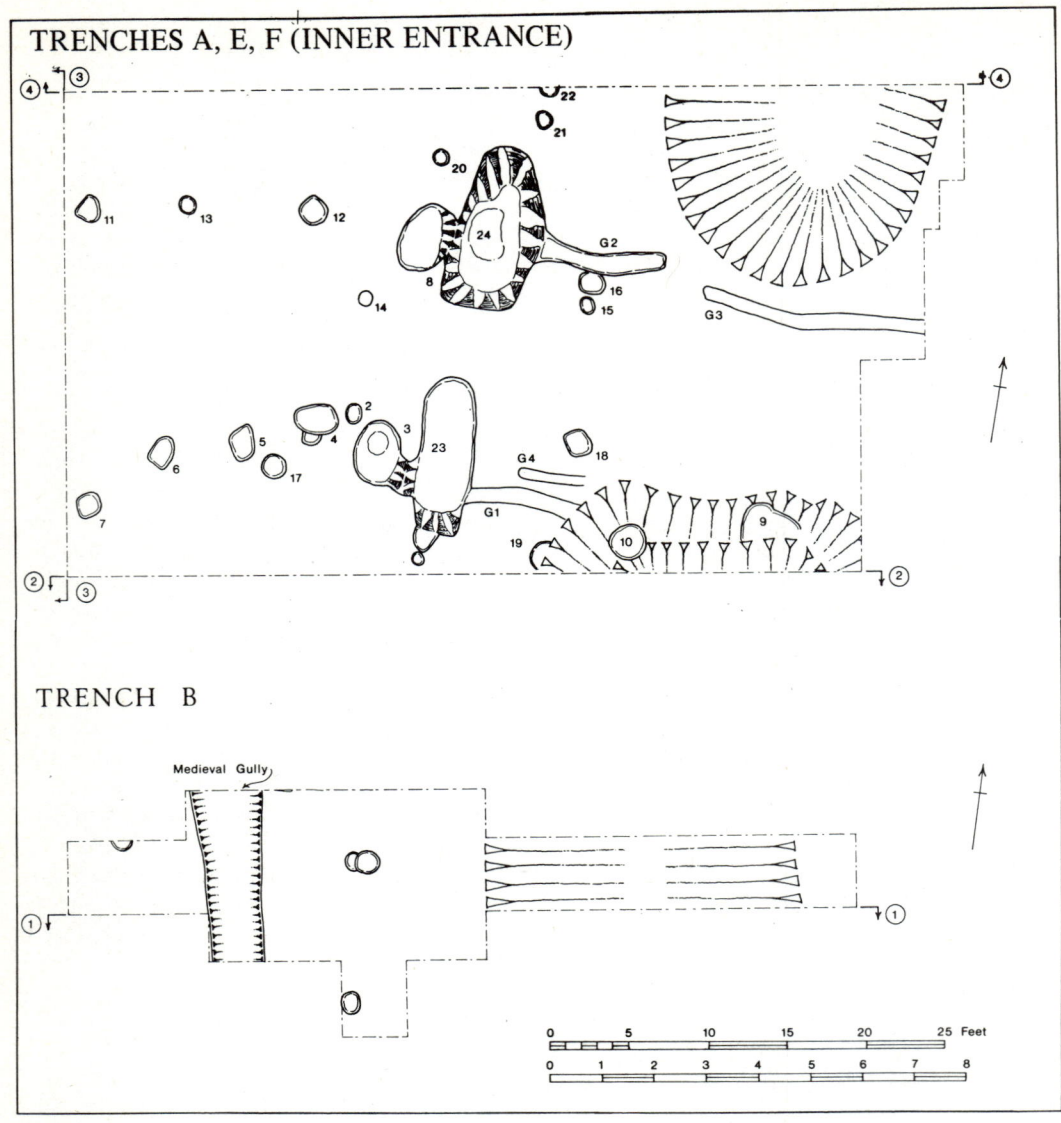

Medieval Gully

0   5   10   15   20   25 Feet

0 1 2 3 4 5 6 7 8

Fig.4   Trenches A, E, F (inner entrance) and trench B (not in correct spatial relationships)

which had been recut; they averaged 9–12 in (0.23–0.30 m) in diameter and 6–9 in (0.15–0.23 m) deep. It seems probable that the posts represent the timber structuring of a box-type rampart, with a row of front revetting timbers set at 9 ft (2.7 m) intervals and a rear revetting placed 15 ft (4.6 m) behind.

In the medieval period the rampart was used as a field boundary defined by a shallow gully containing late 14th century pottery. The field immediately to the east extended across the top of the ditch, the upper part of which gradually became filled with ploughsoil (layer 2). Extensive late medieval ploughing probably accounts for the low level of the surface of the chalk to the east of the ditch compared with that sealed beneath the rampart.

Trench C was a narrow trial trench cut to the south of trench B to establish the position of the ditch, which here was found to be 15 ft (4.6 m) wide at the top. The ditch was excavated to an arbitrary depth of 3 ft (0.90 m) into the top of a layer of chalk-block packing equivalent to layer 9 in trench B. No trace of the rampart survived, nor were any postholes discovered in the trench.

The original entrance: trenches A, E, and F (Figs. 4 and 8 and Pl. IIa)

The plan of the original inner entrance (Fig.4) gives the appearance of a relatively simple structure, but since no

stratigraphy survived, with the exception of that within the individual features, it is impossible to relate one feature with another, except in those cases where a physical relationship existed.

The ditch ends   The south end of the north ditch was totally excavated (Fig.8, section 4). At this point the ditch was 18 ft (5.5 m) wide and 8 ft (2.4 m) deep with sloping sides and a flat bottom. The silting up to the level of the turf line (layer 3a) was largely the result of natural processes: the lenses of soily chalk which had eroded down the west face were interleaved with rather more chalky debris derived from the erosion of the east face. This difference was probably due to the fact that the rampart on the west side may have been built in part of turf. Layer 4 represents a time, before the turf-line had formed, when quantities of occupation debris were tipped into the disused ditch. After the formation of the turf-line, chalky silt continued to wash into the hollow, to be partly sealed by a packing of chalk blocks (layer 3) from among which were recovered sherds of Roman pottery. The final filling of chalky soil (layer 2) probably resulted from medieval ploughing.

The north end of the south ditch was only partly examined, since it did not project far into the excavated area (Fig.8, section 2). Its relationship to postholes 9, 10, and 19 and to gully 1 leaves little doubt that the ditch end, as it now appears, is the result of erosion back from its original lip. The gully leading from gate-post 23 probably once stopped at the ditch lip in a manner similar to the termination of gully 2, on the opposite side of the road, leading from posthole 24. If so, it could be argued that postholes 9 and 10 were dug after the ditch had begun to erode to take uprights supporting a fence continuing the line of that bedded in the gully. An alternative explanation, that the posts pre-date the erosion, is of course possible.

The main gate-posts   The structure of the gate or successive gates would have been supported by the posts set in holes 23 and 3 on the south side of the road, and 24 and 8 on the north side, the physical characteristics of which are evident from Fig.4 and the table below. Clearly, 23 and 24 form one pair, 3 and 8 another. While there is no structural reason why all four posts should not have been standing together (and the stratigraphical relationships were just beyond definite demonstration), the fillings suggest that the two pairs were not contemporary. Both 3 and 8 were packed tight with blocks of chalk after the posts had been removed. The fillings of the two larger holes, 23 and 24, on the other hand, showed that there had been some erosion of their exposed sides, the filling consisting of small chalk lumps mixed with soil, occasional large blocks of displaced chalk packing, some occupation rubbish, and a few small fragments of upper greensand and ferruginous sandstone. All indications are that postholes 23 and 24 were left open after the posts had been removed, to fill up gradually. The fact that pieces of greensand and ferruginous sandstone were found in the filling strongly suggests that the holes remained open after the construction of the east gate had begun, since it was only at this period that foreign stone was brought to the site in any quantity.

The above arguments therefore suggest two phases of gate building. The first gate was represented by postholes 3 and 8, but the posts were later removed and the holes packed before a new gate was erected in postholes 23 and 24.

Gullies   Four gullies or slots were found, running east from the gate posts; they apparently once flanked the causeway between the ditch ends. All four were flat-bottomed and between 6 and 18 in (0.15–0.46 m) deep. They were filled with chalky soil in which no trace of posts could be seen. Both gullies 1 and 2 could be shown to pre-date the gate postholes 23 and 24, while gully 2 appeared to be earlier than posthole 16.

There can be little doubt that gullies 1 and 2 supported palisades or fences designed to prevent access (for livestock or humans) on to the berm between the ditch and bank in the phase when the early gate (postholes 3 and 8) was in existence. When the new gate was built, the fences probably went out of use, but a replacement barrier may have been constructed, based on the posts placed in postholes 16 and 18, which align well with the new gate-posts.

The function and phase of gullies 3 and 4 is more difficult to ascertain, but a fence in gully 3 could have served to prevent jostling animals from falling into the ditch end. It seems likely that gully 4 also once continued past the end of the south ditch before the ditch eroded back, or was recut.

Postholes   In addition to the gate-posts, twenty individual post-holes were found, of which two (4 and 9) show signs of replacement. The details of size and filling may be summarized in list form, in which measurements are given first in inches followed by centimetres in brackets:

Posthole		Depth	Diameter	Filling
1		8 (20)	10 (25)	Medium chalk
2		15 (38)	16 (41)	Large chalk blocks
3	(gate-post)	26 (66)	54 (137)	Large chalk blocks
4a		15 (38)	30 (76)	Medium chalk
4b		13 (33)	17 (43)	Medium chalk
5		15 (38)	24 (61)	Medium chalk
6		18 (46)	17 (43)	Large chalk blocks
7		6 (15)	18 (46)	Large chalk blocks
8	(gate-post)	27 (69)	54 (137)	Large chalk blocks
9		6 + (15)	?	Medium chalk filling post-void. Large chalk packing around.
10		6 + (15)	24 (61)	ditto
11		6 (15)	24 (61)	Large chalk blocks
12		15 (38)	17 (43)	Medium-large chalk blocks
13		15 (38)	15 (38)	Large chalk-block packing
14		6 (15)	12 (30)	Medium chalk
15		7 (18)	12 (30)	Medium chalk
16		15 (38)	18 (46)	Small-medium chalk
17		21 (53)	16 (41)	Small-medium chalk
18		10 (25)	18 (46)	Medium chalk
19		–	24 (61)	Large chalk blocks
20		8 (20)	12 (30)	Medium chalk
21		8 (20)	12 (30)	Medium chalk
22		15 (38)	?	Medium chalk
23	(gate-post)	24 (61)	irregular (Fig.4)	Medium-fine chalk silting
24	(gate-post)	25 (63)	irregular (Fig.4)	Medium-fine chalk silting

From the above description it will be seen that some of the posts were deliberately packed with large chalk blocks, while others contained fillings of smaller chalk fragments. In view of the supposed two-phase structure of the gate, it remains a distinct possibility that the chalk-packed posts represent an early stage in the revetment of the rampart ends. If so, the fact that only a few other posts are recorded in the area would imply that no extensive revetting was maintained in the second phase.

The roadway   The roadway which ran through the gates did not exceed 9 ft (2.74 m) in width. No trace of metalling survived but a slight hollow had been created by traffic (Fig.8, section 3).

The junction of the cross-ditch and the main fort ditch: trenches D and G (Figs.5, 9)

Because of the sharp westward curve of the cross-ditch, trench D, which was designed to be at the point of junction between the cross-ditch and the main ditch, proved to lie too far east. Trench G was therefore dug next to it, the complexity of the features uncovered requiring the trench to be further extended to the south. For the sake of simplicity, the features will be described as far as possible in chronological order.

The end of the original cross-ditch   The original ditch end was discovered extending for a distance of 20 ft (c. 6 m) to the south of the later south ditch of the fort. When seen in complete section (Fig.9 section 9) it was flat-bottomed, measuring 6 ft (1.83 m) deep by 11 ft (3.35 m) wide. It had been allowed to silt up naturally (layers 4 and

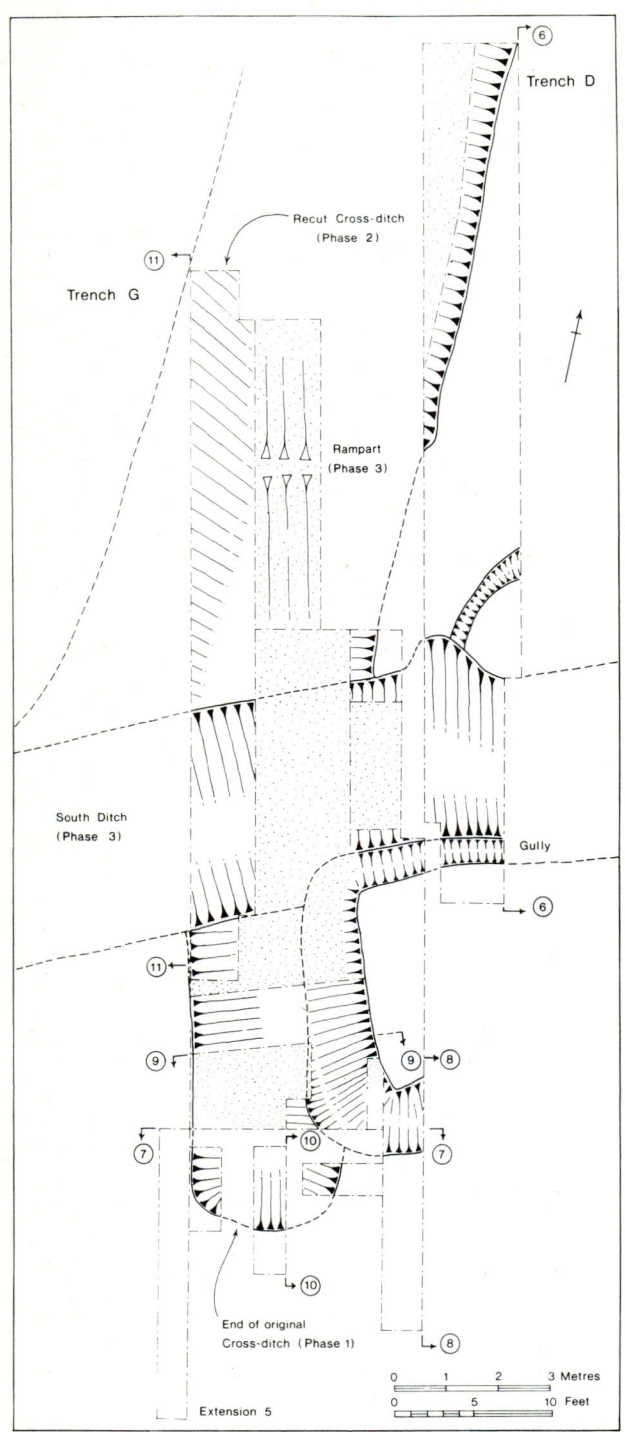

Fig. 5   Site 2: junction area

15) before a thick layer of freshly quarried chalk blocks (layer 18) was packed across the top, probably at the time when the later south ditch was dug across it.

The recutting of the cross-ditch   Figure 5 shows that the cross-ditch to the north of the later south ditch was considerably wider and deeper than the original ditch end to the south and, moreover, appears to be aligned further to the west. The only reasonable explanation for this is that the ditch was at some time recut either ending at least 20 ft (6 m) short of the original end or, more probably, extending around the hill to enclose the western summit. Part of

trench G cut obliquely through the silting of the ditch (section 11, layer 9). The upper part of the silt was also exposed in trench D (section 6, layer 9), where it can be seen to be sealed by the tail of the later rampart (layer 8). No complete section was obtained in this area, but the section provided by trench B can be regarded as typical of the cross-ditch in its recut stage.

The later south ditch and rampart   After the recut cross-ditch had had time to accumulate silt, the enclosed area of the fort was greatly extended to the east by the construction of a new rampart and ditch which, around the eastern end of the hill, was the first defence to be erected. To the west of the cross-ditch the surviving defences either belonged wholly to this late phase or were a recut version of an existing ditch — it depends upon which interpretation of the extent of the recutting of the cross-ditch is correct (see preceding paragraph).

The later south ditch crossed trenches D and G, where two complete sections of it were obtained (Fig.9, sections 6 and 11). In trench D (section 6) the rampart had been almost entirely removed by ploughing, with the exception of a spill of chalk blocks from its tail preserved beneath the turf-line in the hollow of the old cross-ditch. In trench G, however, where the south ditch cut almost at right-angles through the partially silted cross-ditch, a sloping revetment of turf and chalk had been constructed, partly to retain the loose silt of the truncated ditch and partly to revet tips of chalk rubble thrown in to fill the ditch and form a basis for the rampart (section 11, layers 10 and 4). It was probably at this time that the chalk packing of the original cross-ditch end was undertaken to create a stable outer lip for the new ditch (see above).

The south ditch was eventually allowed to silt up naturally (section 6, layers 10, 11; section 11, layers 19, 20, 21), the only difference between the two sections being that in trench G the ditch silt contained more soil, which must have derived from the erosion of the turf revetting.

The gullies   Figure 5 gives the plan of a gully which was found to enclose three sides of a square or rectangular area approximately 12 ft (3.66 m) across. The gully was cut into the packing of the original cross-ditch end and ran parallel to the side of the later south ditch, the relationship between the two having been destroyed by later ploughing. It therefore post-dates the recutting of the cross-ditch and may be later than the construction of the main south ditch, but, apart from being sealed by medieval ploughsoil, it is otherwise undated. Its sections and relationships can best be appreciated from Fig.9: its filling consisted largely of chalk from the erosion of the sides (trench G, layers 8, 16; trench D, layer 12).

A further but unrelated length of gully was discovered in trench D (section 6, layer 4). It is undated but could equally as well pre-date the south ditch as post-date it. The fact that the ditch side had eroded back at this point suggests that the gully may have been earlier than the ditch. Its relationship to the 'square gully' is unknown.

Ploughing   In the medieval period the north edge of the south ditch seems to have been used as a headland giving rise to the creation of a negative lynchet which gradually filled with ploughsoil and hill-wash (section 6, layer 3; section 11, layer 2).

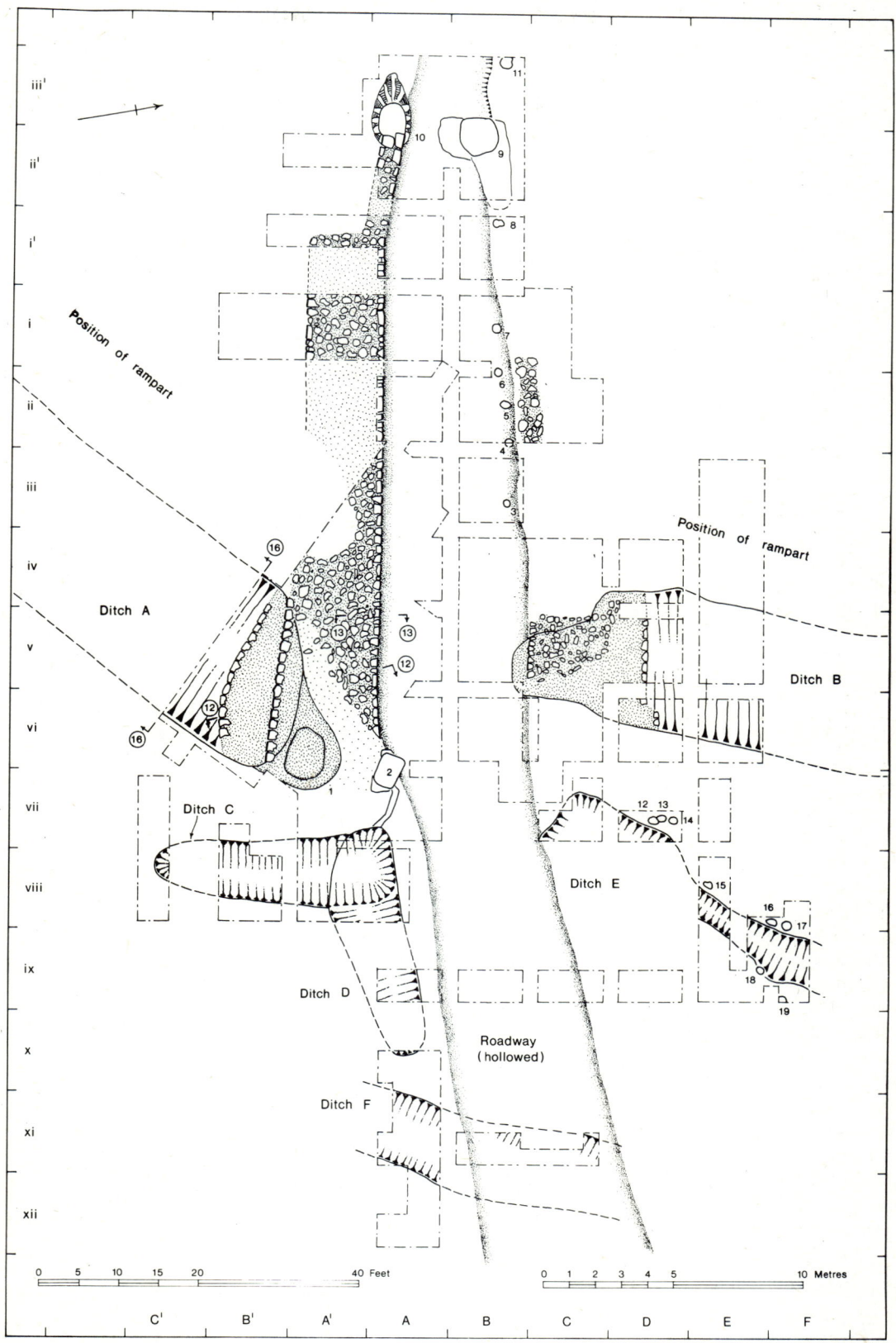

iii'
ii'
i'
i
ii   Position of rampart
iii
iv
        Ditch A
v
vi
vii   Ditch C
viii
ix   Ditch D
x   Roadway
        (hollowed)
xi   Ditch F
xii

10
11
9
8
7
6
5
4
3
2
16
13
12
1

Position of rampart
Ditch B
12 13
14
Ditch E
15
16
17
18
19

0 5 10 15 20   40 Feet

0 1 2 3 4 5   10 Metres

C'   B'   A'   A   B   C   D   E   F

Fig. 6   East entrance

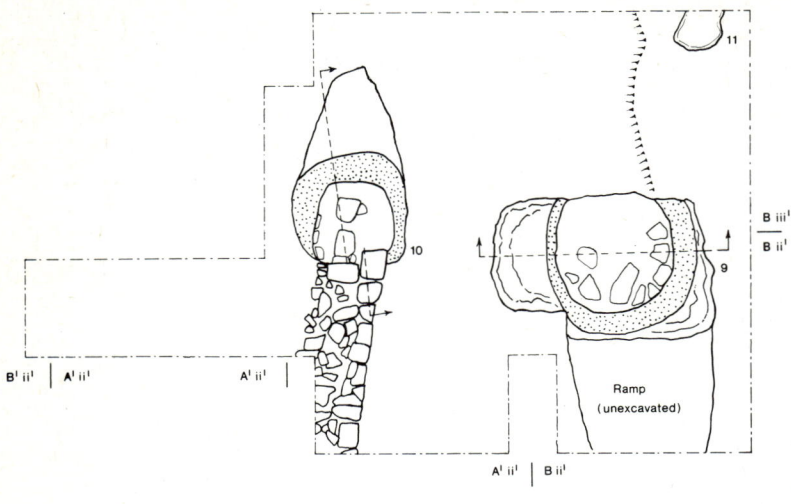

Fig.7 Plan of the east gate and sections of gate postholes

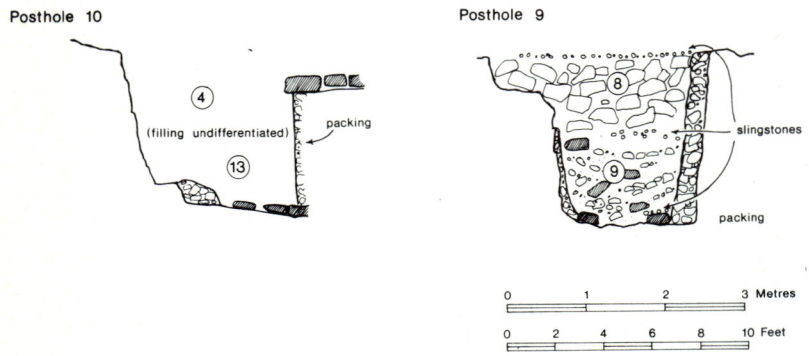

Posthole 10

Posthole 9

0   1   2   3 Metres

0   2   4   6   8   10 Feet

The east entrance (Figs.6, 10–13)

Although no trace of the east entrance survives on the surface, having been totally obscured by medieval ploughing, a
trackway can be made out running up the gentle east flank
of the hill and a similar length is visible within the fort continuing much the same line. Brightwell and Taylor assumed
that the entrance lay on this line to the south of the small
copse in which they had found the fort ditch curving round
to the south. Their single trial trench ran along the roadway
between the ditch ends, thus proving them to be correct.

The excavation of 1956, which was designed to examine
the entrance in detail, began with a trench cut at right-angles
across the south ditch. This was later expanded to explore
the entire ditch end and part of the foundations of an adjacent wall which flanked the entrance roadway in its latest
phase. When the more extended programme of work began
in 1957 it was decided to excavate within a 10 ft grid system aligned with the face of the flanking wall. The following season saw the further expansion of the area examined
within the confines of the same grid. The results of the
work are summarized on Fig.6.

The ends of the main ditch (Figs.10, 11; Plate IIb)

The end of the south ditch, examined in 1956, was 20 ft
(6 m) wide and 7 ft (2.1 m) deep. After a little silt had accumulated (section 16, layers 10 and 11), a drystone wall
had been built across the ditch and the space between it and
the ditch end packed with chalk rubble to the level of the
surrounding ground surface. The wall was composed largely
of blocks·of ferruginous sandstone derived from the Lower

Greensand outcrops in the Weald. Although the individual
stones were roughly dressed, no consistent attempt had been
made to lay them in regular courses, as will be apparent
from the elevation diagram (Fig.10, section 14).

From the surviving evidence it cannot be shown how extensively the ditch had silted before the blocking wall was
put up, but since the base of the wall was bedded in silt and
the wall appeared to revet undisturbed layers of primary
silt, it is clear that some erosion had taken place and that
not all of the detritus had been removed. In front of the
wall, however, extensive cleaning out had been undertaken
and it remains a strong possibility that the ditch was kept
clear of debris by regular scourings until the wall was
allowed to collapse.

The lowest layers in the ditch represented the primary
silt: layer 11 (on section 16) derived from the erosion of
the outer ditch side, while layer 10 resulted from the
erosion of the inner slope and possibly a turf-faced rampart
above. The period was short-lived: thereafter the wall
collapsed (or was destroyed), giving rise to a mass of
tumbled rubble and chalk (layer 9). Layer 8, which
followed, represented a secondary silting composed of
shattered chalk mixed with soil deriving from natural processes of erosion and weathering, which continued to give
rise to finer-textured silting (layer 7), until an angle of rest
was reached, at which stage a turf line formed (layer 6).
The subsequent layers were created by ploughing.

The north ditch end proved to have been treated in
much the same way, but the details are somewhat clearer
(Fig.11). After a considerable amount of silt had accumulated (section 17, layer 6), the end was blocked off by a

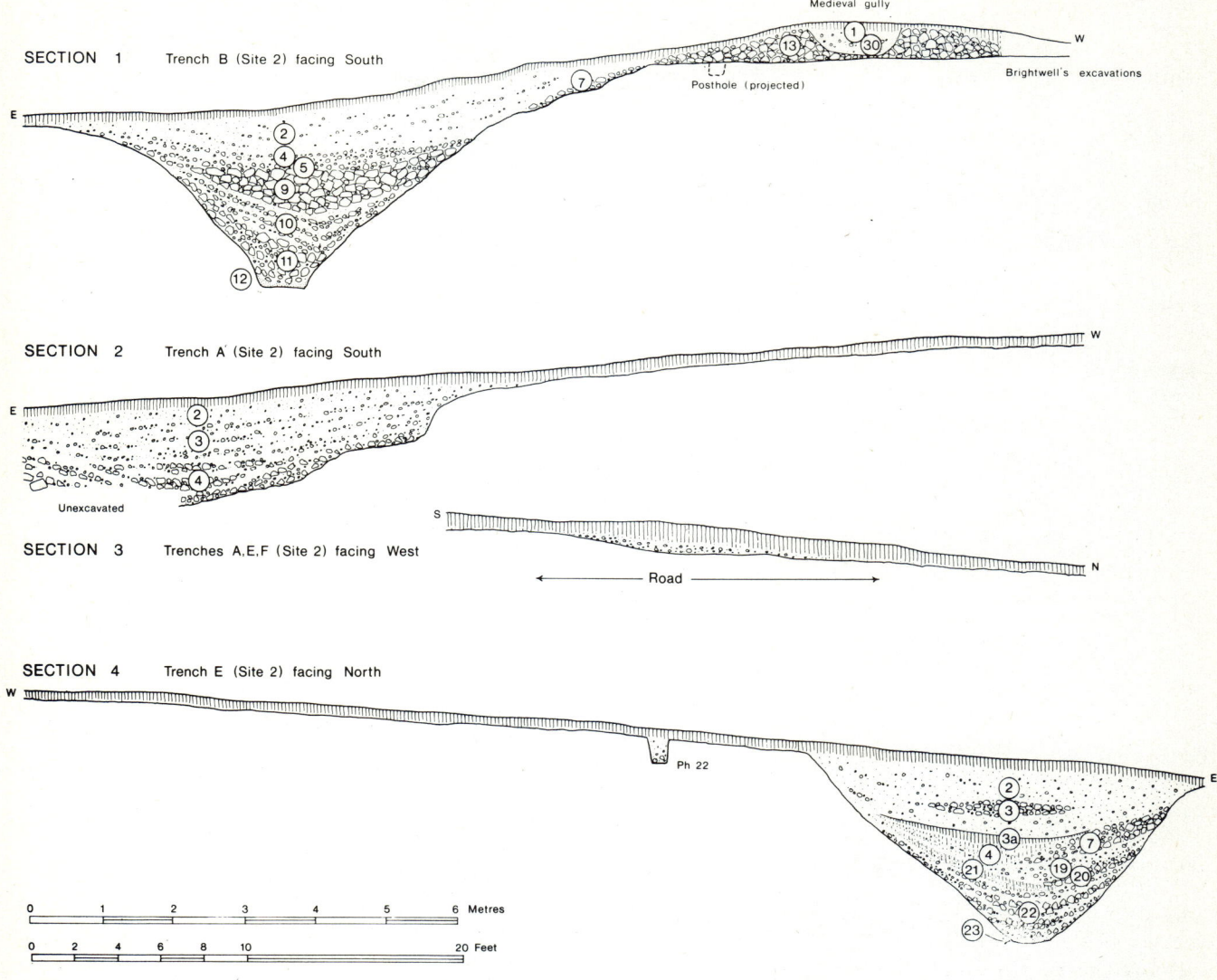

SECTION 1   Trench B (Site 2) facing South

Medieval gully

W

Brightwell's excavations

Posthole (projected)

SECTION 2   Trench A (Site 2) facing South

W

E

Unexcavated

SECTION 3   Trenches A,E,F (Site 2) facing West

S

N

←——— Road ———→

SECTION 4   Trench E (Site 2) facing North

W

Ph 22

E

0   1   2   3   4   5   6 Metres

0   2   4   6   8   10   20 Feet

Fig.8   Sections of cross-ditch and its entrance

cross-wall of similar construction to that built in the south ditch end, erected after the ditch had been substantially cleared out. The space behind the wall and above the silt was filled with tightly packed fresh chalk rubble (section 17, layer 5) to the level of the surrounding surface.

Section 17 clearly shows that the level of the ditch bottom in front of the blocking wall was about 1 ft (0.3 m) lower than the level beneath and behind the wall, one implication being that after the wall had been built the ditch was cleared out, possibly on several occasions, each operation resulting in the gradual lowering of the bottom. The ditch was virtually clear of silt when the wall collapsed, giving rise to the mass of tumbled blocks (Dvi, layer 4; Evi, layer 5). Thereafter, by a process of natural silting, layers 4b and 4 formed, later to be sealed by a turf-line (layer 3b) which marked an angle of rest. Above this the finely textured silt (layer 3) may represent the first phase of ploughing, followed by the formation of another turf-line (layer 3a), before the onset of an extensive phase of ploughing in the medieval period which filled the remaining hollow of the ditch with chalky soil (layer 2).

Post-holes and road contemporary with the original ditch ends

Figure 6 shows two excrescences, one attached to each of the inner ends of the main ditch. The southern example, when excavated, proved to be a large posthole (ph 1) measuring 4 ft 6 in x 6 ft 6 in (1.37 x 1.98 m) at the top, by 3 ft (0.91 m) deep. Its southern edge had eroded into the ditch end. The filling was entirely of fresh chalk rubble, apparently contemporary with the chalk packing behind the revetting wall in the ditch.

Close by, another posthole was found (ph 2) measuring 3 ft by 4 ft 3 in (0.91 x 1.30 m) at the top and 2 ft (0.61 m) deep. Some original packing of chalk blocks was found along the east side, suggesting that a post had once stood here before being removed and the void becoming filled with looser packed chalk blocks. The fact that the filling contained no stone blocks at all but was sealed by a layer of mixed stone and chalk derived from the erosion of the later stone wall (Fig.10, section 15) strongly suggests that this posthole belongs to the pre-wall phase and is thus broadly

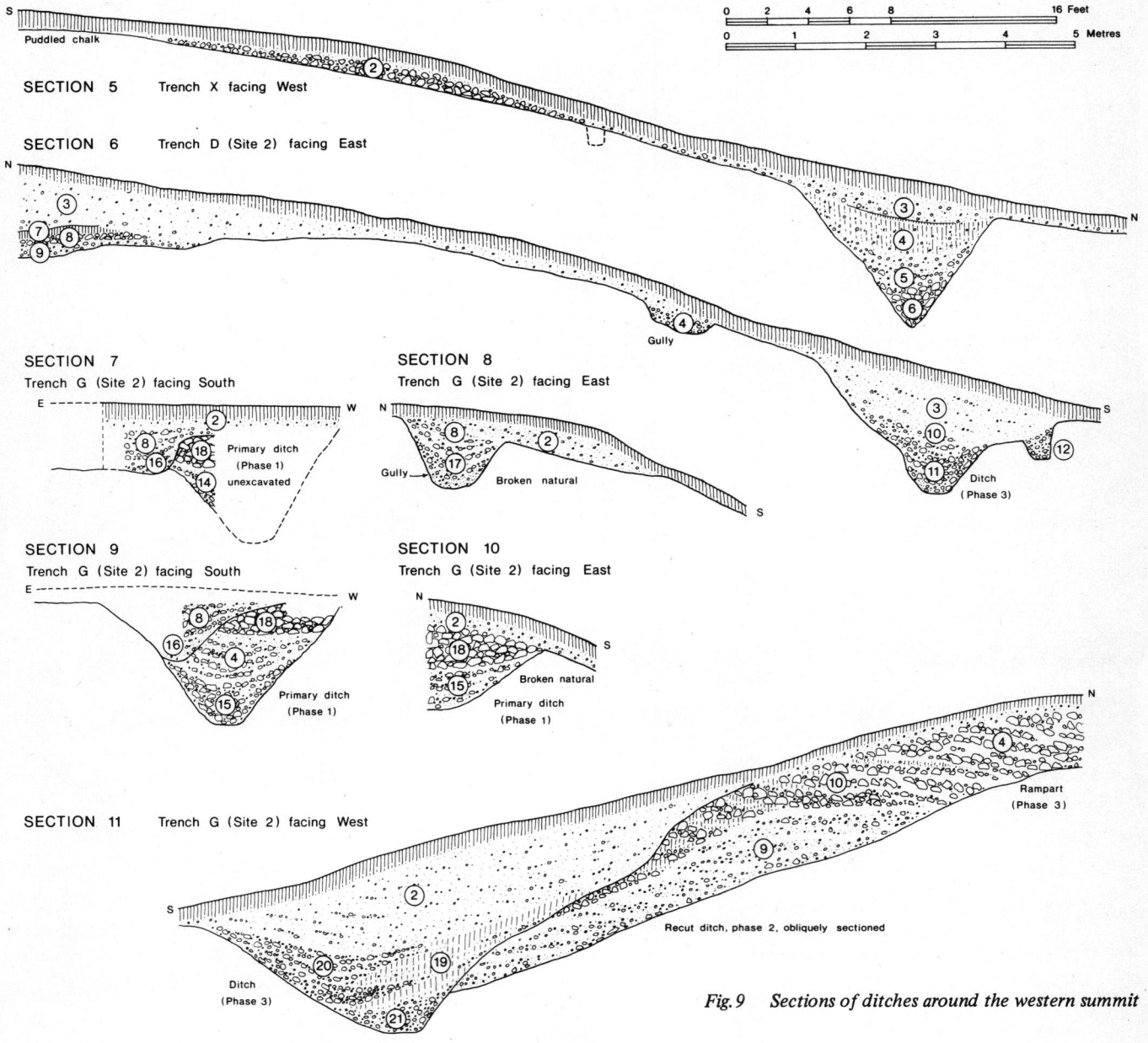

SECTION 5   Trench X facing West

SECTION 6   Trench D (Site 2) facing East

SECTION 7
Trench G (Site 2) facing South

SECTION 8
Trench G (Site 2) facing East

SECTION 9
Trench G (Site 2) facing South

SECTION 10
Trench G (Site 2) facing East

SECTION 11   Trench G (Site 2) facing West

Fig. 9   Sections of ditches around the western summit

contemporary with posthole 1 and the original phase of the ditches.

The protrusion extending south from the original north ditch end was not excavated below its packing of chalk rubble, which extended continuously up to the revetting wall. Nothing is therefore known of the original structures in this area, but a general similarity to the south ditch end would suggest the existence of a large posthole.

The details of the gate and road belonging to the first phase of the entrance were largely obscured or destroyed by the flanking walls and hollowed road of the second phase to be described below. In trench **AV**, however, a small section of the later wall was removed to expose part of the puddled surface of the early road (Fig.10, section 13), the south edge of which was at this point 4 ft (1.22 m) south of the later road. It seems likely that this early road passed diagonally between the slightly overlapped ditch ends.

The only structural evidence which might be thought to belong to the early gate was a row of postholes in trenches BI ', BI, BII, and BIII, details of which are given below. Although they appear to relate in plan to the edge of the later road, they were seen to pre-date the wear caused by the traffic of the second period. It is impossible on such slight evidence to say how, if at all, these posts functioned in relation to the original gate structure. Indeed, the possibility remains that they may have belonged to the early stages of the later gate before the road had worn its deep hollow.

Postholes flanking road (measurements in inches and in centimetres in brackets)

Posthole	Diameter	Depth	Other details
3	10 x 7 (25 x 18)	8 (20)	
4	6 x 9 (15 x 23)	7 (18)	
5	6 x 10 (15 x 25)	9 (23)	
6	10 (25)	11 (28)	
7	12 (30)	24 (61)	oblique: leaning north-east
8	14 x 9 (36 x 23)	9 (23)	

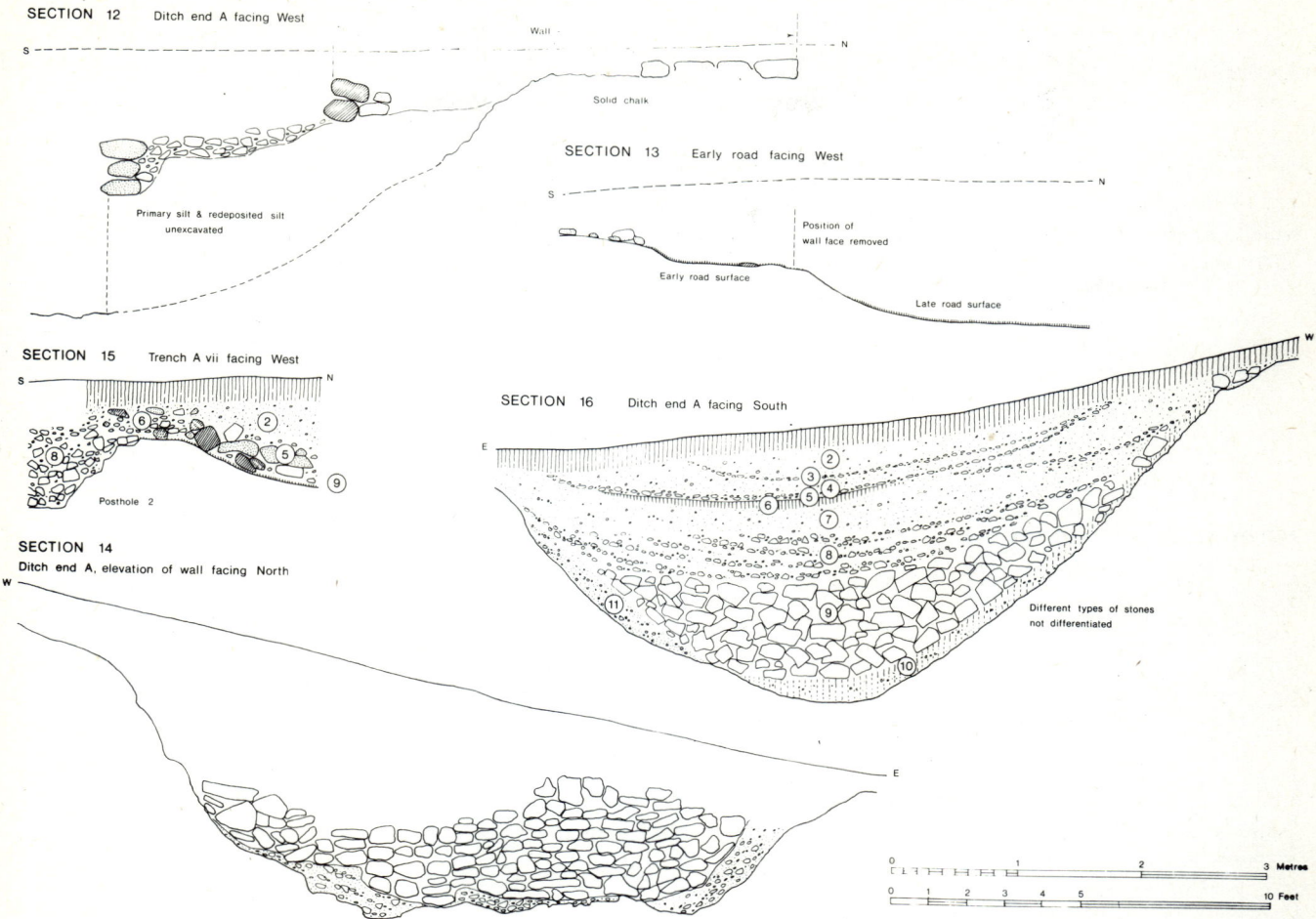

Fig.10   Sections of the ditch ends at the east entrance

The inturned flanking walls and latest gate (Fig.6)

The filling of the ditch ends was undertaken to widen the entrance gap in order to accommodate a slightly realigned roadway flanked by massive drystone walls. The roadway was examined for most of its length together with the well preserved foundations of the south wall; of the north wall little survived.

The south wall was traced for a distance of 75 ft (23 m) from the site of the main gate to its easternmost surviving position. If, as seems likely, it originally ended on line with ditch C it would once have been some 85 ft (26 m) in length. The width averaged 10 ft (3 m), but gradually expanded to 15 ft (4.6 m) at its eastern end. At the west end it narrowed abruptly to 3 ft (0.91 m) for the last 13 ft (3.96 m) of its length. The form of the wall is best appreciated from the plan (Fig.6), the sections (Fig.12), and the illustrations in Plates IV and V. The external faces were built of roughly squared blocks of Upper Greensand and ferruginous sandstone, set dry and uncoursed to create a vertical face which now survives to a maximum height of 2 ft (0.61 m). Between the faces rubble, including some chalk and flint, was loosely packed. The wall face which passed over the filled-up south ditch end is of particular interest, for the builders had deliberately chosen ironstone blocks of a distinctive purple colour for the basal course, evidently to create a visual effect (Plate IIb). It is not impossible that similar attention to decorative detail was lavished on the upper part of the wall, which no longer survives.

The treatment of the east end of the wall remains obscure, since medieval ploughing has reduced everything hereabouts to the natural chalk surface, but ditch C appears to have been dug to protect the approach to the projecting end face. Although it might be thought that posthole 2 was integral with the wall, its deliberate filling of chalk blocks, without any stone of the kind of which the wall was built, would argue that it preceded the construction of the wall.

The north wall was considerably reduced by ploughing, but a patch of stones with a length of facing blocks survived in the slight hollow caused by the consolidation of the filling of the north ditch end. A further area of stonework remained in position in the area sectioned by trenches CII (Plate IVb). The treatment of the eastern end of the wall is unknown, but ditch E is considerably earlier and bears no relation to it.

The main gate-posts (Fig.7)

At the inner end of the two flanking walls were placed the two main gate-posts, only 7 ft (2.13 m) apart.

Posthole 9 (Plate IIIb) measured approximately 6 ft (1.83 m) in diameter and 7 ft (2.13 m) in depth. The post which it supported originally measured 5 ft (1.52 m) in diameter at ground level, tapering to 4 ft (1.22 m) at the bottom; it had been chocked up on ironstone blocks placed

11

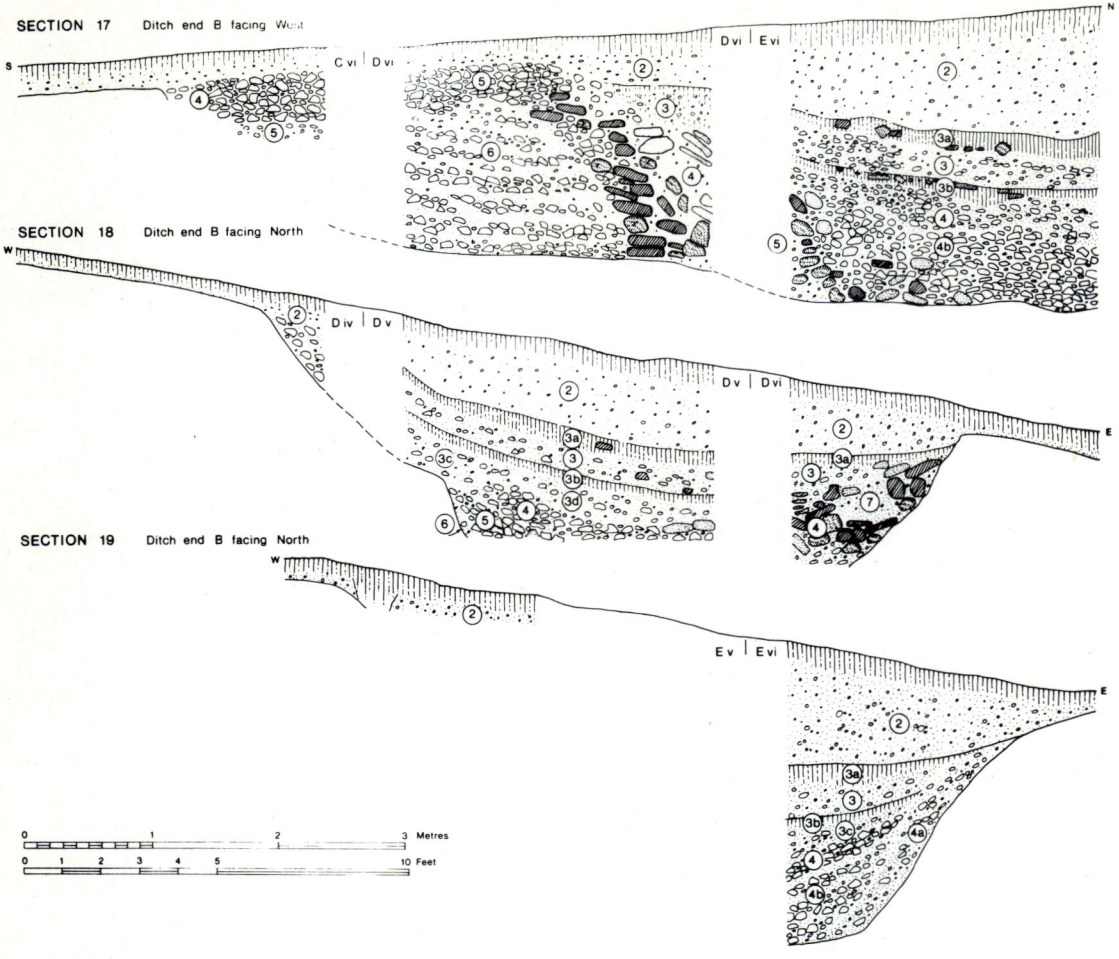

SECTION 17   Ditch end B facing West

SECTION 18   Ditch end B facing North

SECTION 19   Ditch end B facing North

0   1   2   3 Metres

0 1 2 3 4 5   10 Feet

Fig.11   Sections of the ditch ends at the east entrance

in the pit bottom and was packed around with rammed chalk rubble. The erection of so large a post would undoubtedly have been a difficult task, but this was facilitated by the provision of a sloping ramp extending east from the main pit. Once the post was in position, the hollow of the ramp was packed with chalk and rubble. Immediately adjacent to the west side of the post was a layer of slingstones numbering about 180.

The filling of the hole suggests that the post had been deliberately uprooted. Almost immediately 28 slingstones fell in from the adjacent layer; then the chalk packing partially collapsed to give rise to layer 9 filling the hole to a depth of 3 ft (0.9 m). At this stage a further 40 slingstones slipped in. Thereafter the upper part of the hole was filled with a mass of sandstone blocks from the adjacent walls, which had either tumbled in or were thrown down deliberately (layer 8).

Posthole 10 (Plate IIIa) measured approximately 5 ft (1.5 m) in diameter and 6 ft (1.83 m) deep, supporting a post of diameter 3 ft (0.9 m). The post had been lowered into the pit down a sloping ramp extending from its west side, and had been chocked in position on a number of ironstone blocks placed on the pit bottom. Once upright, the

space between the timber and the pit side was packed with rammed chalk and the south wall was laid across the packing up to the face of the post.

Post 10, like post 9, seems to have been deliberately uprooted. The void was immediately filled with a loose tumble of stone blocks from the adjacent wall (layer 13). The upper filling of the hole (layer 4), though similar, contained rather more soil and debris derived from nearby occupation levels.

The form of the gate itself is beyond recovery, but it was evidently a massive structure. The larger diameter of post 9 might suggest that the gate was hinged in some way to it. If so, it would have swung back into the fort, possibly into the scarped recess which had been cut into the bedrock. It is even possible that posthole 11, some 8 in (0.20 m) deep, served as a stop or an attachment post.

The Roadway (Fig.12)

Between the walls the roadway measured 18 ft (5.5 m) wide at the east end, narrowing to 7 ft (2.1 m) between the gateposts. It had been subjected to heavy traffic, resulting in the formation of a hollow-way worn, on average, to a depth of 2 ft (0.61 m) below the original chalk level. Even clear

12

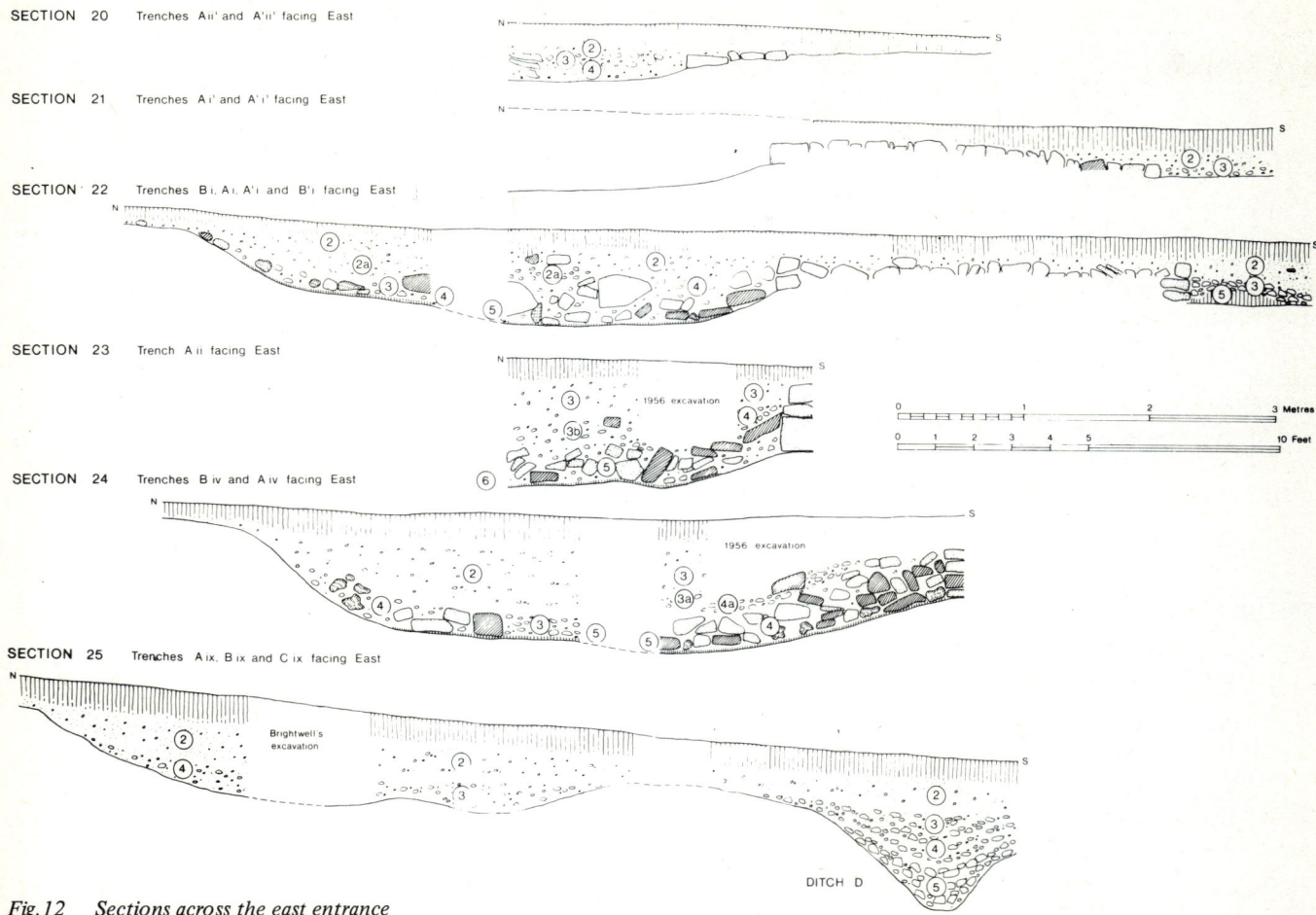

SECTION 20   Trenches A ii' and A'ii' facing East

SECTION 21   Trenches A i' and A'i' facing East

SECTION 22   Trenches B i, A i, A'i and B'i facing East

SECTION 23   Trench A ii facing East

SECTION 24   Trenches B iv and A iv facing East

SECTION 25   Trenches A ix, B ix and C ix facing East

DITCH D

Fig.12   Sections across the east entrance

of the construction of the entrance works a noticeable hollow had been created. The road was not metalled, but its puddled surface contained chips of stones that had flaked off the adjacent walls.

Immediately above the road surface, where it ran between the inturned walls, lay a tumbled mass of stone, undoubtedly derived from the walls, which must have been deposited immediately after the road had ceased to be used and before any silting or erosion had taken place. Although it is impossible to prove, the impression given is that the stones were thrown down from the wall rather than deriving from the gradual decay of the structure. Thereafter the remaining hollow filled with chalk and soil largely as the result of ploughing activity.

The ditches in front of the entrance

Four ditches were discovered in front of the entrance, called here ditches C, D, E, and F (Fig.6).

Ditch C (Fig.13, sections 27 and 29), 8 ft (2.4 m) wide and 3 ft (0.91 m) deep, ran for a distance of 30 ft (9.14 m) in front of the east end of the south flanking wall and presumably served to protect the approach to it. It can be shown to be later than ditch D (see below). It had silted up naturally almost to half of its depth (section 27, layers 10 and 4) before stones from the wall began to collapse into it (layer 3). The tumble was eventually sealed by ploughsoil (layer 2).

Ditch D (Fig.13, sections 28 and 29; Fig.12, section 25)

ran parallel to the approach road for a distance of 28 ft (8.5 m). At its eastern (downhill) end it was only 2 ft 6 in (0.76 m) deep, but increased to 5 ft (1.52 m) in depth at the uphill end (see sections 25, 28, 29).

It appears to have silted up naturally almost to the top before ditch C was dug, incorporating its western end. At the point of overlap the lower silt of ditch D had been dug out and the space packed with large, freshly quarried chalk blocks (section 29 layer 9) to the level of the bottom of ditch D. For this reason ditch D is likely to belong to the first phase of the entrance and is therefore broadly contemporary with postholes 1 and 2.

Ditch E lies to the east of the main north ditch end. It was roughly cut and is irregular in profile, and plan, varying from 3 to 5 ft 6 in (0.9–1.68 m) wide and about 3 ft (0.9 m) deep. The filling was completely natural, consisting entirely of chalk and silt that had eroded in from the sides. It bore no stratigraphical relationship to any other feature, the only dating evidence being a few sherds of pottery from the silt.

On both sides a number of postholes were recovered, all filled with fine to medium chalk silt:

Posthole	Diameter	Depth
12	35 x 14 (89 x 36)	14 (36)
13	33 x 11 (84 x 28)	10 (25)
14	16 x 11 (41 x 28)	13 (33)
15	11 x 10 (28 x 25)	8 (20)

13

16	19 x 10 (48 x 25)	6 (15)	
17	17 x 16 (43 x 41)	6 (15)	
18	9 x 9 (23 x 23)	32 (81)	appeared to cut the ditch silt.
19	c.10 (c.25)	4 (10)	

Although posthole 18 appears to post-date the ditch fill, the relationship of the others to the ditch is unknown.

Ditch F (Fig.13, section 26). Ditch F was traced across the line later taken by the roadway leading to the gate: it was flat-bottomed with near-vertical sides, averaging 8 ft (2.44 m) across by 2 ft (0.61 m) deep. The lower silting was natural (section 26, layers 5, 9), but above this a layer of medium-sized chalk blocks had been thrown in (layers 3 and 6), possibly to consolidate the filling prior to the setting out of the entrance so that the approach road could pass unhindered.

SMALL FINDS (Fig.14)

1 *Pin and spring of an iron fibula very much corroded.* The spring is of an 8-coil type wrapped around an iron rod: the cord is external. There is little to be gained from detailed typological discussion, except to say that the brooch is clearly a La Tène type but of uncertain phase.
From the east entrance, trench Dv, layer 4 – ditch silt in front of the blocking wall. (The brooch cannot now be traced but a drawing survived from which the present illustration is taken).

2 *Part of a bronze terret ring.* The type with simple lipped decoration is well known in southern Britain, occurring, for example, at Glastonbury (Bulleid and Gray 1911, pl. XLIV), where comparable examples from Bawdrip (Somerset), Stanwick and Arras (Yorks.), Hunsbury (Northants), and Hagbourne Hill (Berks.) are briefly discussed. To these might be added the terret from Hod Hill (Dorset) (Richmond 1968, Fig.31), which provides a very close parallel to the Torberry fragment. The date lies in the 1st century BC or early 1st century AD. From the 1956 excavation in the medieval ploughsoil sealing the fill of the south ditch-end.

3 *Lead bead or weight eccentrically perforated.* For similar example from Glastonbury, see Bulleid and Gray 1911, pl. XLV. From the 1956 excavation in the tumble of stone representing the destruction of the phase 4 entrance.

4 *Bronze ring lacking distinctive characteristics.* From trench B (sectioning the cross-defence) in posthole in south section. It is possible that the ring fell into the void after the post had rotted or been removed.

5 *Part of a bracelet of Kimmeridge shale.* The shale was quarried in Kimmeridge, on the Isle of Purbeck, and there worked into bracelets (Calkin 1949, 1953; Cunliffe and Phillipson, 1968). Distribution of the raw material or finished products, most commonly bracelets, was widespread in the pre-Roman Iron Age, reaching as far as All Cannings Cross in the north and the Caburn in the east. From Trench 9, layer 8 – the filling of the 'rectangular' gully.

6 *Fragment of a glass bead of deep blue colour.* The surface was once decorated with a spiral of white glass, which has since largely disappeared, leaving only a groove to mark its position. Blue glass beads with inset spirals occur sporadically in most parts of Britain. They have been discussed and partially listed by Bulleid and Gray (1917, 353–9) and Ward-Perkins (1944, 165–6). An example has recently been found at Danebury, Hants, in a 3rd or 2nd century BC context.

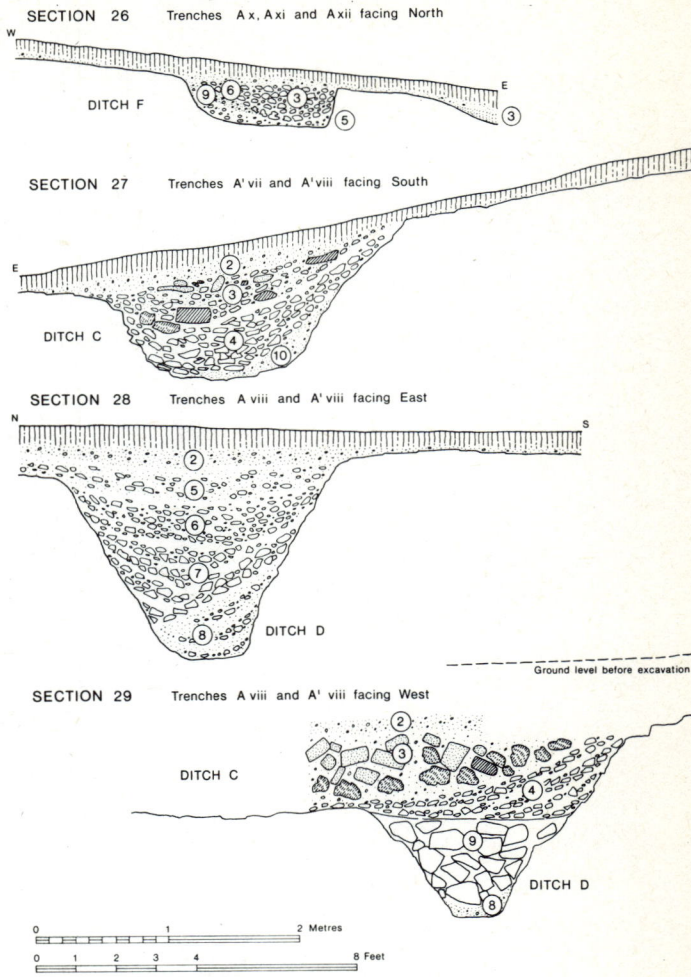

SECTION 26 Trenches A x, A xi and A xii facing North

SECTION 27 Trenches A'vii and A'viii facing South

SECTION 28 Trenches A viii and A' viii facing East

SECTION 29 Trenches A viii and A' viii facing West

Fig.13 Sections of the outworks at the east entrance

From the 1956 excavation in the tumble of stones representing the destruction of the phase 4 entrance.

7 *Fragment of decorated long bone, possibly once part of a handle.* From Trench AIII', layer 3: chalk rubble beneath ploughsoil.

8 *Decorated bone weaving or plucking comb of well known type.* Found by Brightwell in a pit behind the cross-defence. The comb is now in the Barbican House Museum, Lewes. It is redrawn here after Curwen 1954, Fig.82.

9 *Spindle whorl in a well fired flint-gritted fabric.* Found by Brightwell: location uncertain.

10 *Bottom stone of a rotary quern of Upper Greensand.* The shape is typical of querns of the later pre-Roman Iron Age. From Trench Ai' layer 3: tumbled stone rubble lying on the road surface.

THE POTTERY

The excavations were designed to study the structural sequence of the hillfort defences and not to examine the nature of the contemporary occupation layers. For this reason, groups of closely stratified pottery from pits were

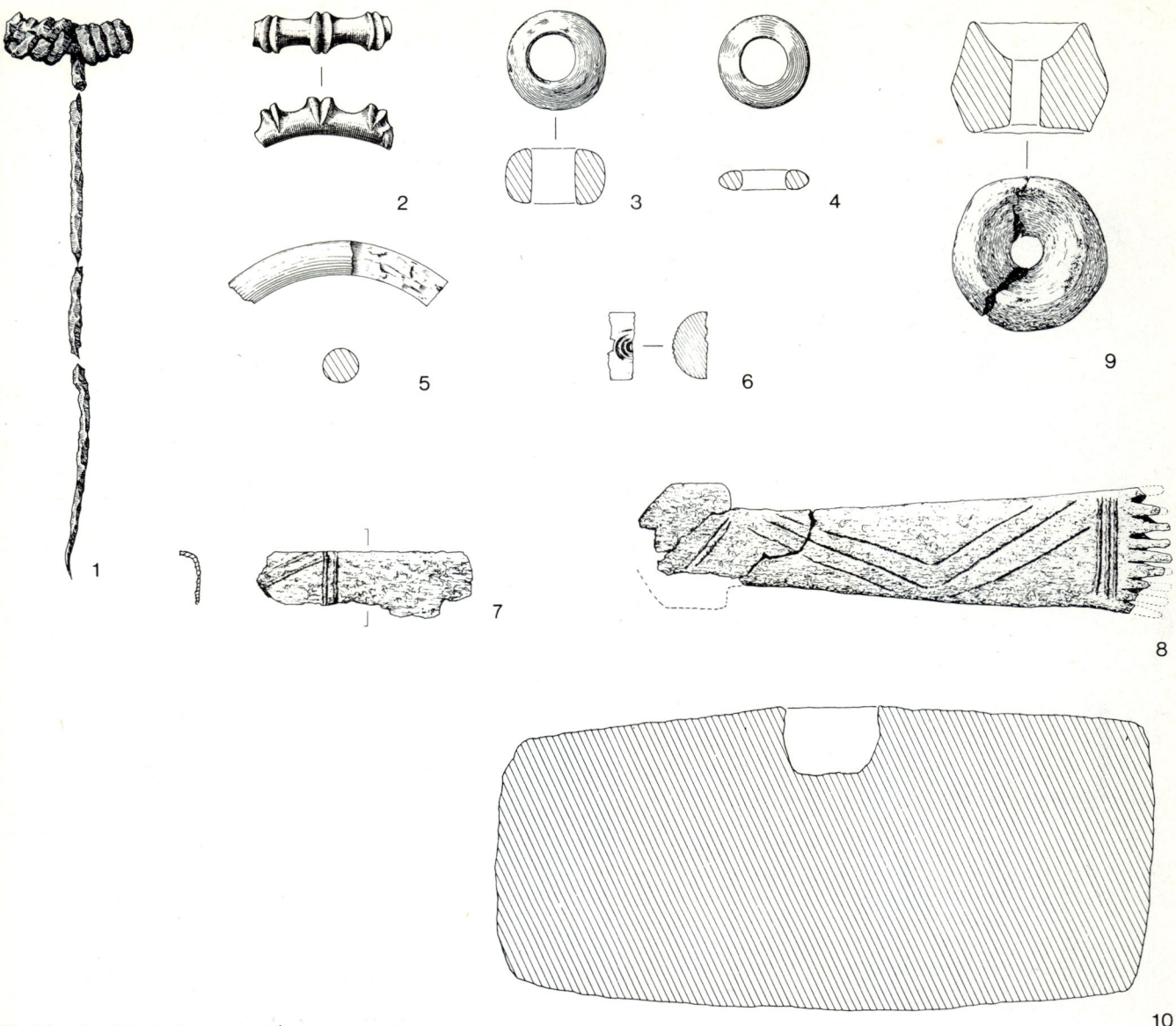

Fig.14   Small finds 1—9, scale 2/3; 10, scale 1/3

not recovered. In five situations, however, all related to the defences, reasonably large assemblages came to light: these account for a substantial number of the illustrated sherds and are published below in their stratified groups, to which are added a selection of isolated sherds from other contexts.

The policy adopted in the following report is to illustrate all rims and decorated sherds in Figs.15—22 and to offer a quantitative summary of all sherds related to their stratigraphical contexts. To obviate repetition of fabric descriptions, the fabrics have been divided into seven coded classes as follows. In the case of the illustrated sherds the type of fabric is noted in the caption.

Fabric A	Sandy clay matrix tempered with coarse unsorted crushed flint grits, some very large. Roughly finished surface. Variously fired black to red.
Fabric B	Sandy clay matrix, tempered with medium-sized crushed flint grits. Roughly finished surface. Variously fired black to red.
Fabric C	Sandy clay matrix tempered with fine—medium crushed flint grits. Well smoothed surface. Always from large jars with walls in excess of 1 cm. thick.
Fabric D	Smooth, soft, sandy fabric. Occasional flint grits. Smoothed surface fired to brown or dark grey.

Fabric E	Fine sandy matrix tempered with fine—medium crushed flint grits. Burnished surfaces sometimes decorated. Usually fired to dark grey or black.
Fabric F	Fine hard sandy fabric occasionally tempered with flint grits. Burnished surface; usually fired dark grey or black.
Fabric G	Hard grey sandy ware.

Descriptions and locations of the illustrated pottery (Figs.15—22)

Group 1: Pottery associated with the cross-defence (Fig.15)

1 From the rampart; trench B, layer 13

2 From a posthole in the rampart; trench B, layer 15

3 From the secondary silt of the ditch north of the entrance; trench E, layer 7

4 From the secondary silt of the ditch; trench B, layer 10

5 From the primary silt of the ditch; trench B, layer 12

6 From ploughsoil above the ditch silt; trench B, layer 2

7 From the silt of the ditch; trench G, layer 9

8 From the silt of the ditch; trench D, layer 9

9 From the silt of the ditch; trench D, layer 11.

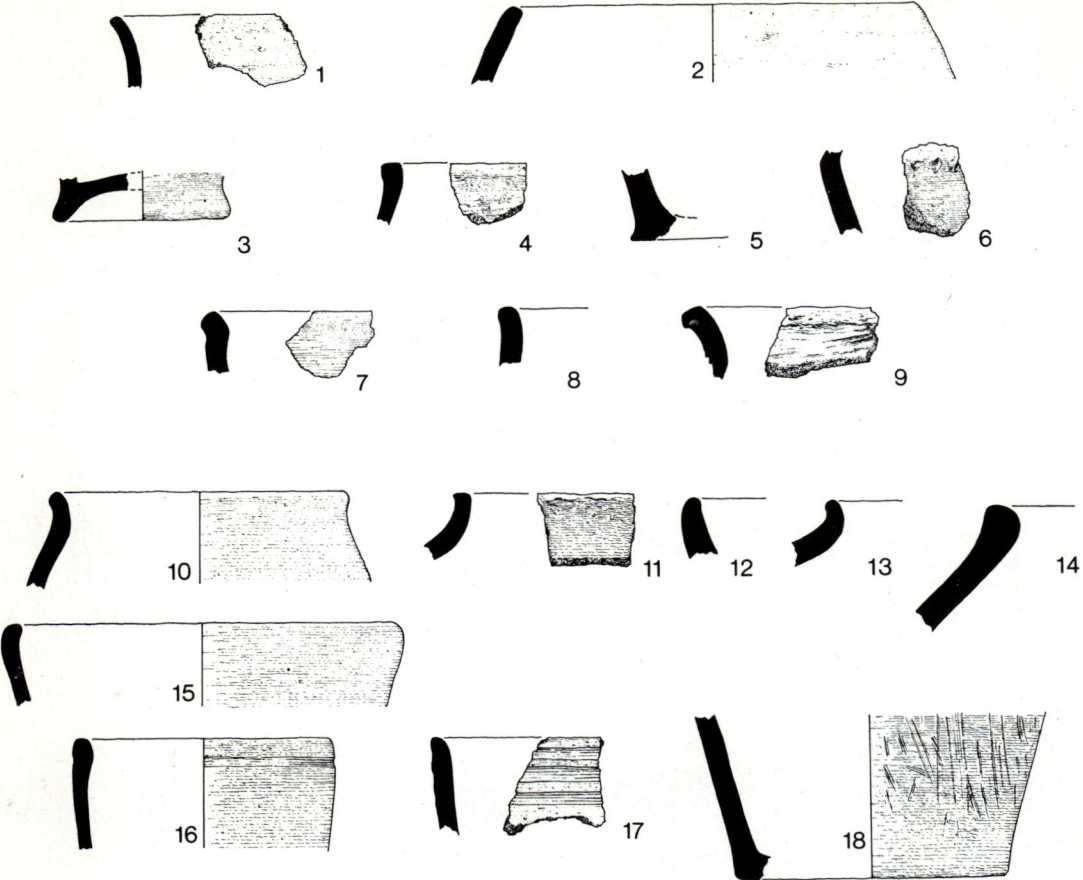

Fig.15   Pottery: scale ¹/₃. Nos. 1–9; group 1 associated with the cross-ditch; 10–18: group 2 from the rectangular gully cut into the packing of the cross-ditch end. Fabrics: fabric A, No. 5; fabric B, Nos. 1, 6, 9, 11, 13, 18; fabric E, Nos. 2–4, 7, 8, 10, 12, 14–17

Group 2: Pottery from the rectangular gully (Fig.15)

10–18   from trench G, layer 8.
This group must post-date the abandonment of the early cross-ditch end.

Group 3: Pottery from the rampart constructed across the recut cross-ditch (Fig.16)

19–34   from trench G, layers 7, 10, 11, 12.

35–42   from trench G, layer 2. Derived largely from the erosion of the rampart layers: thus the majority of the sherds were probably once incorporated in these layers.

The rampart layers were composed partly of chalk dug out of the ditch and partly from turves and soil derived, presumably, from the inside of the fort. The pottery, most of which was in the soil layers, therefore represents the occupation of the site up to the time of the extension of the fort, i.e. periods 0–2 in terms of the sequence offered on pp. 25–6.

Group 4: Pottery from a tip of occupation debris in the partially silted-up ditch end of the cross-defence (Fig.17–18)

43–65   from trench E, layer 4.

The occupation rubbish is likely to have accumulated in the ditch end, either as the result of deliberate tipping or from a limited *in situ* occupation in the hollow presented by the partially filled ditch. In either case it must represent a period when the ditch was no longer functioning as a defence. It therefore belongs to period 3 or 4, when the extended fort was in use. The alternative, that it represents occupation after the main fort gate was destroyed, while possible is unlikely.

Group 5: Pottery from above the road leading to the east gate (Fig.19)

66–71   from trench B IX, layer 2.

The group probably represents rubbish accumulating after the gate had been destroyed and the road abandoned. Alternatively it may have eroded in from occupation layers beside the road.

Group 6: Pottery from tips of occupation debris in the end of the ditch on the north side of the east entrance (Fig.19)

72–82   from trench CV, layer 4.

This group must represent a period transitional between phases 3 and 4, that is, after the fort had been extended but before the gate had been rebuilt: it was sealed by the chalk rubble thrown into the ditch end to create a level platform for the inturned gate wall.

Group 7: Pottery from the filling of the gate posthole 9 (Fig.20)

83–97   all from the filling of the posthole, Trench AIII′, layers 4 and 13.

Since the posthole was deliberately filled in a short space of time, the pottery, most of which is in large non-abraded sherds, is likely to represent a near-contemporary group, dating broadly to the time of the fort's destruction. It is therefore in all probability slightly later than group 3 unless, of course, the sherds were derived from an old rubbish tip nearby and thrown into the posthole.

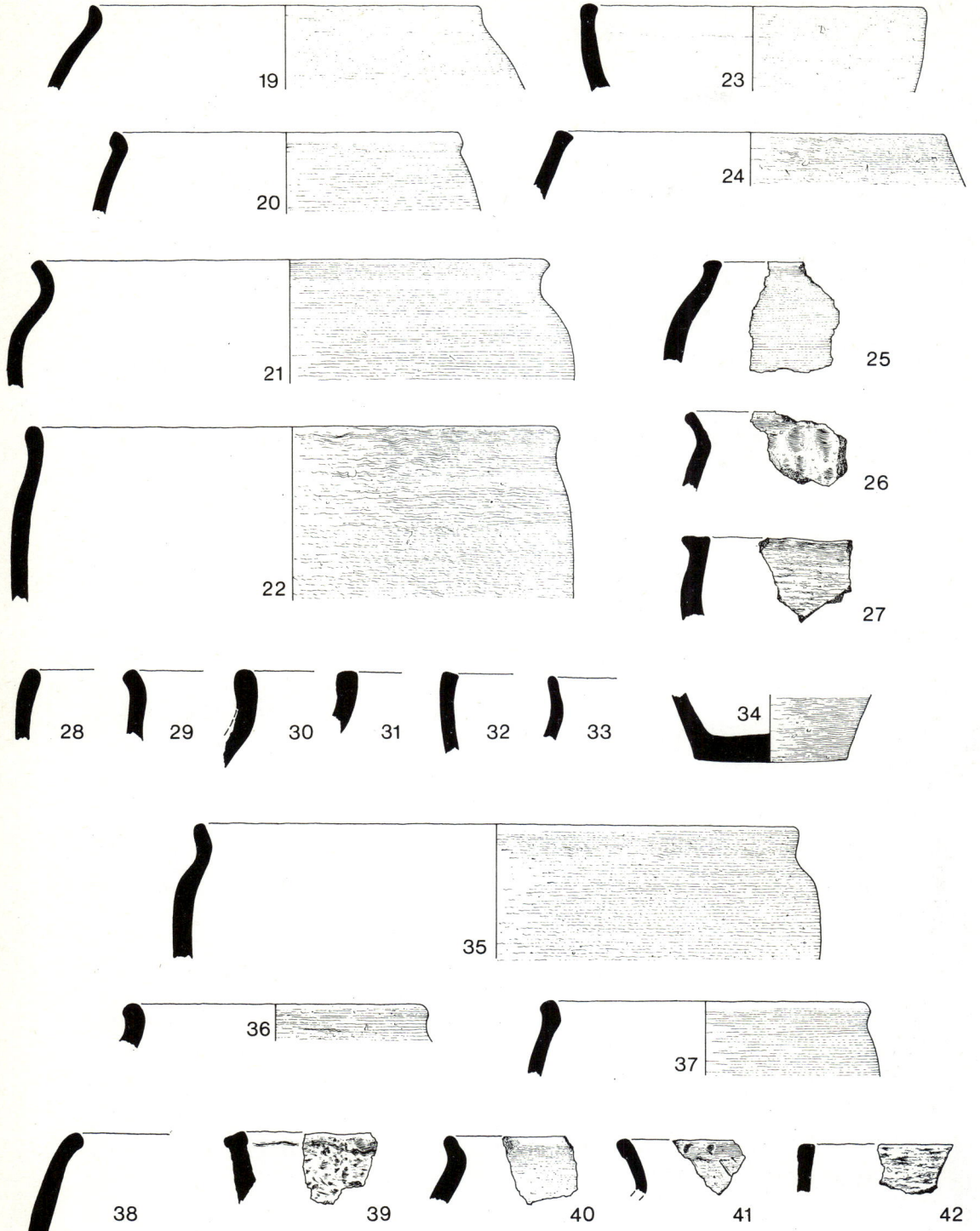

Fig.16   *Pottery: scale $\frac{1}{3}$. Nos. 19–42, group 3 from the rampart constructed across the cross-ditch and the silt derived from it.*
Fabrics: fabric A, No. 31; fabric B, Nos. 22, 26–8, 33–5, 38, 40–2; fabric D, No. 39; fabric E, Nos. 19–21, 23–5, 30, 32, 36, 37; fabric G, No. 29

Group 8: Miscellaneous pottery from various unstratified positions, mainly ploughsoil (Fig.21)

98–106   from ploughsoil and rubble.

107–108 from Brightwell's excavation, location uncertain.

The sherds selected for illustration here are representative of the earliest phase of occupation on the hill. Most of them were pro-

bably brought to the surface and redeposited during the period of medieval ploughing.

Group 9: Pottery of the late pre-Roman Iron Age (Atrebatic) (Fig.21)

109–113 from trench B'VIII, layer 2, a layer of silty chalk in the top of ditch C, post-dating the collapse of the inturned wall.

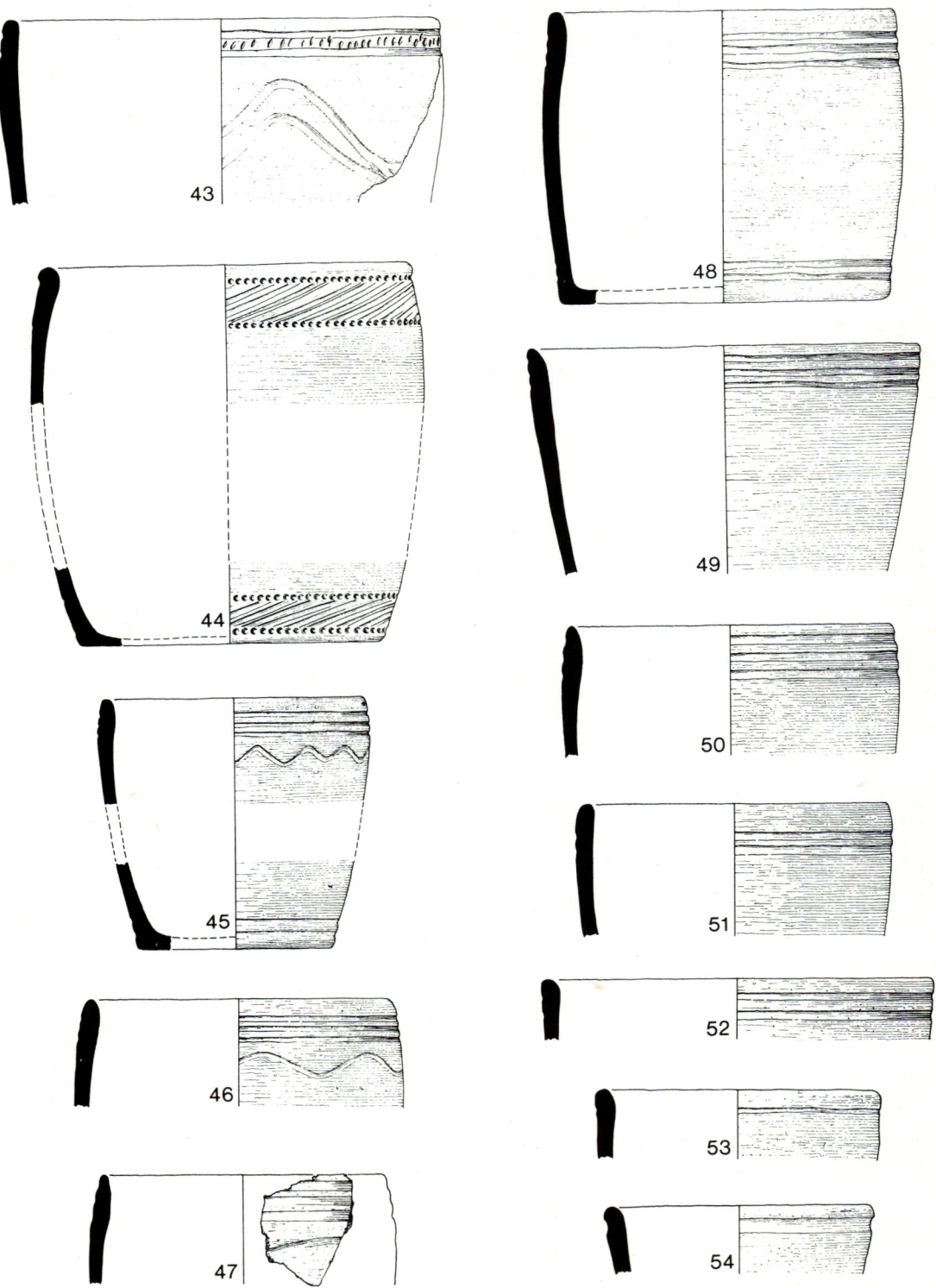

Fig.17   Pottery: scale $^1/_3$. Nos. 43–54, group 4 from rubbish layer in silted-up cross-ditch end
Fabrics: fabric D, Nos. 43, 45, 56; fabric E, Nos. 44, 47–54

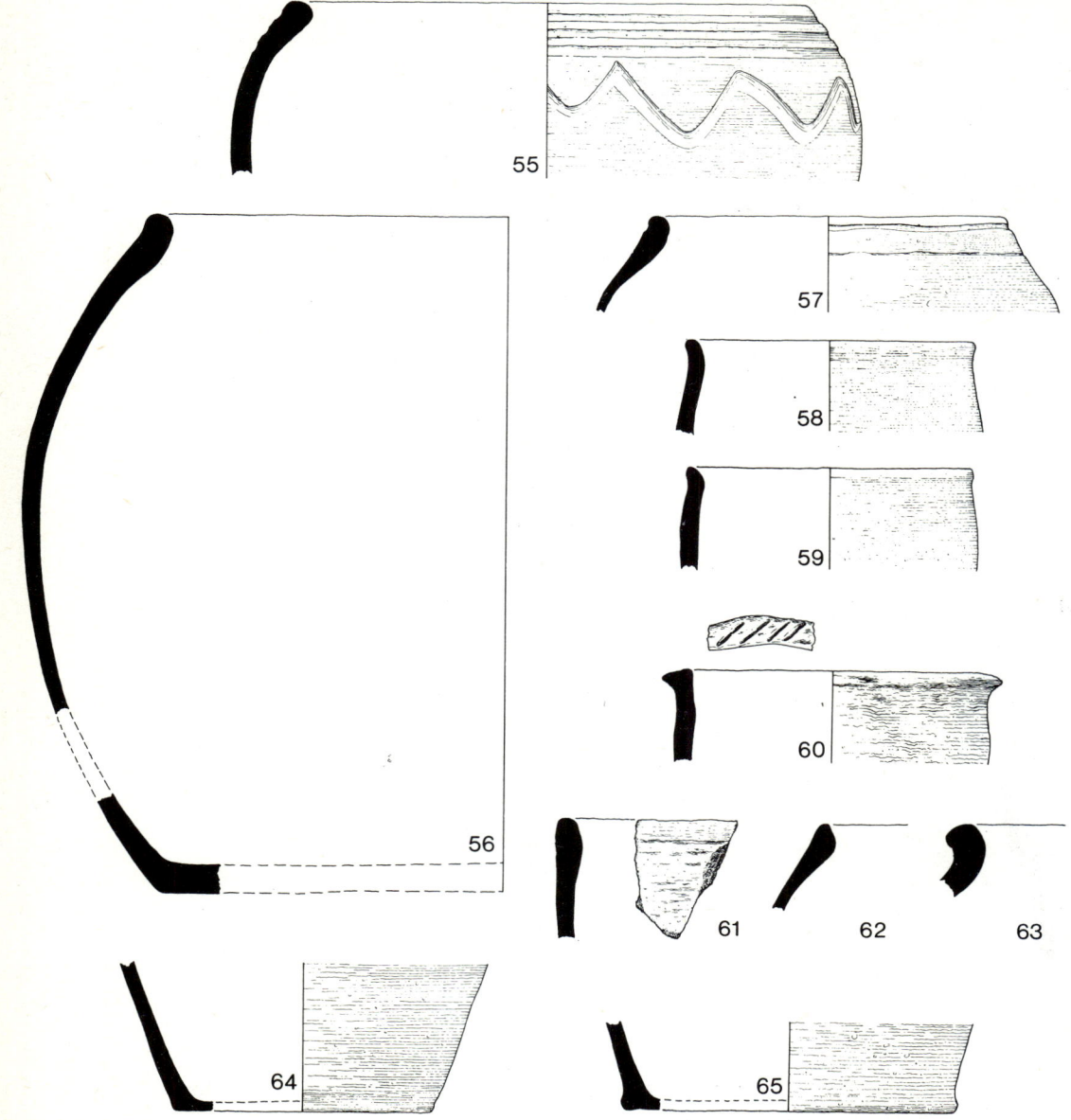

Fig.18   Pottery: scale ¹/₃. Nos. 55–65, group 4 (continued), from rubbish layer in silted-up cross-ditch end
Fabrics: fabric B, No. 60; fabric E, Nos. 55–9, 61–5

114   from trench CXI, layer 3.

The group consists of vessels typical of the mid-1st century AD. Nos. 109–113 are in the native tradition, No. 114 is a local copy of a Gallo-Belgic platter.

Group 10: Pottery from the medieval gully cut into the rampart of the cross-bank (Fig.22)

115   Pitcher in a fine grey sandy ware fired red on the inside and glazed externally with a glassy green glaze which has begun to crystallize. From trench B, layer 30.

116   Cooking pot, wheel-turned, in a fine-hard sandy ware fired to a brownish colour.

The gully was probably dug when the hill was being divided for ploughing in the late medieval period.

Summary of all pottery related to context

The following lists include all sherds from stratified positions, arranged in trench and layer order. The illustrated vessels are noted only by their publication number: body sherds are quantified according to the fabric groups, listed above (p.15); prefixed by f (abbreviation for 'fabric').

Trenches across cross-defence

Trench B	layer 2	Drawn, no.6 Also misc. body sherds.
	layers 4 & 5	body sherds: 5 fA; 5 fB; 3 fC
	layer 10	Drawn, no.4 Body sherds 16 fA; 6 fB; 5 fD; 3 fE.
	layer 12	Drawn, no.5
	layer 13	Drawn, no.1 Body sherds 3 fB; 1 fE.
	layer 15	Drawn, no.2
Trench C	layers 5 & 6	Body sherds 73 fB.

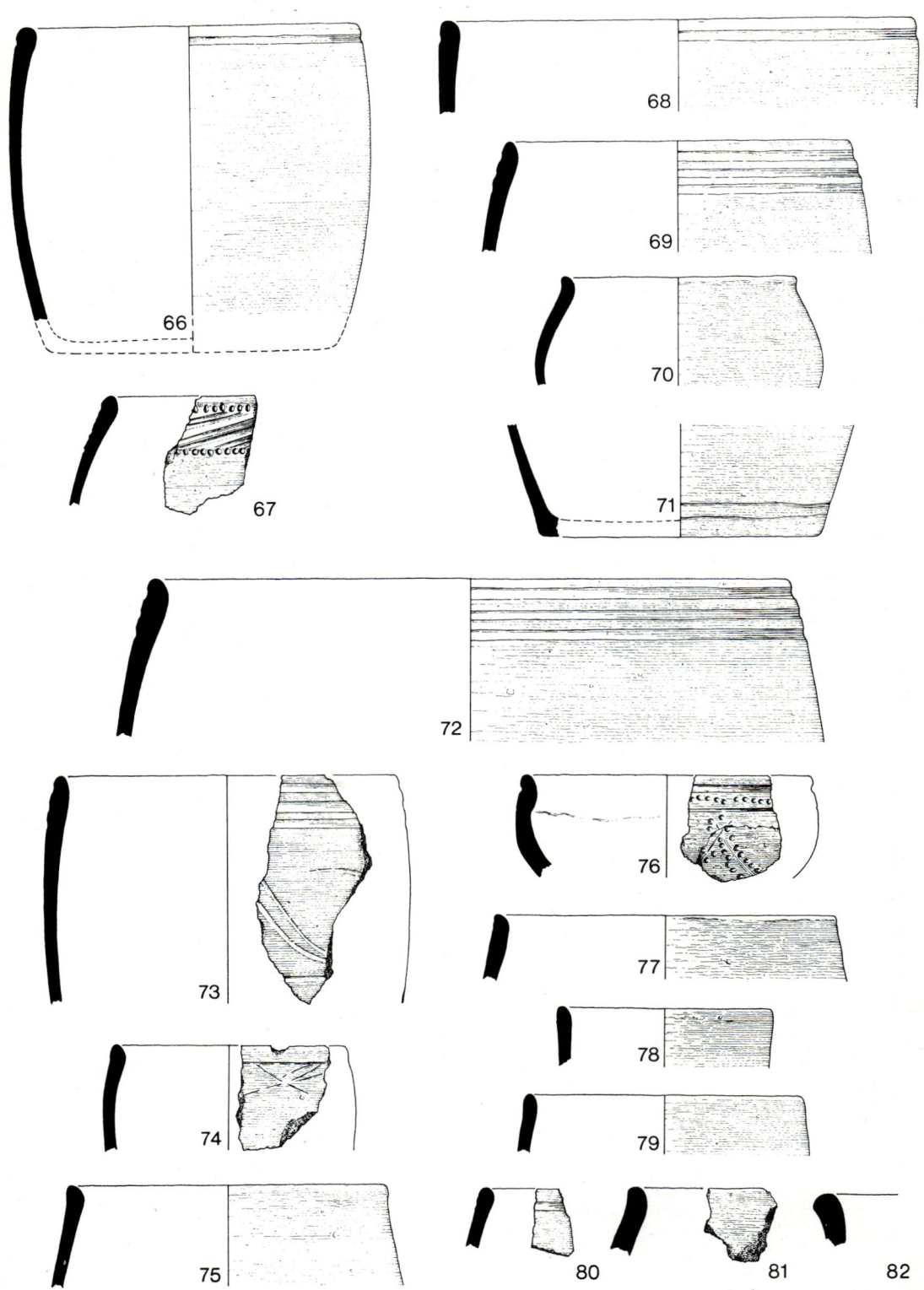

Fig. 19   Pottery: scale ¹/₃. Nos. 66–71, group 5 from above road leading to east gate: Nos. 72–82, group 5, from debris in end of ditch at east gate
Fabrics: fabric E, Nos. 66–74, 76–9, 81–2; fabric E, Nos. 75, 80

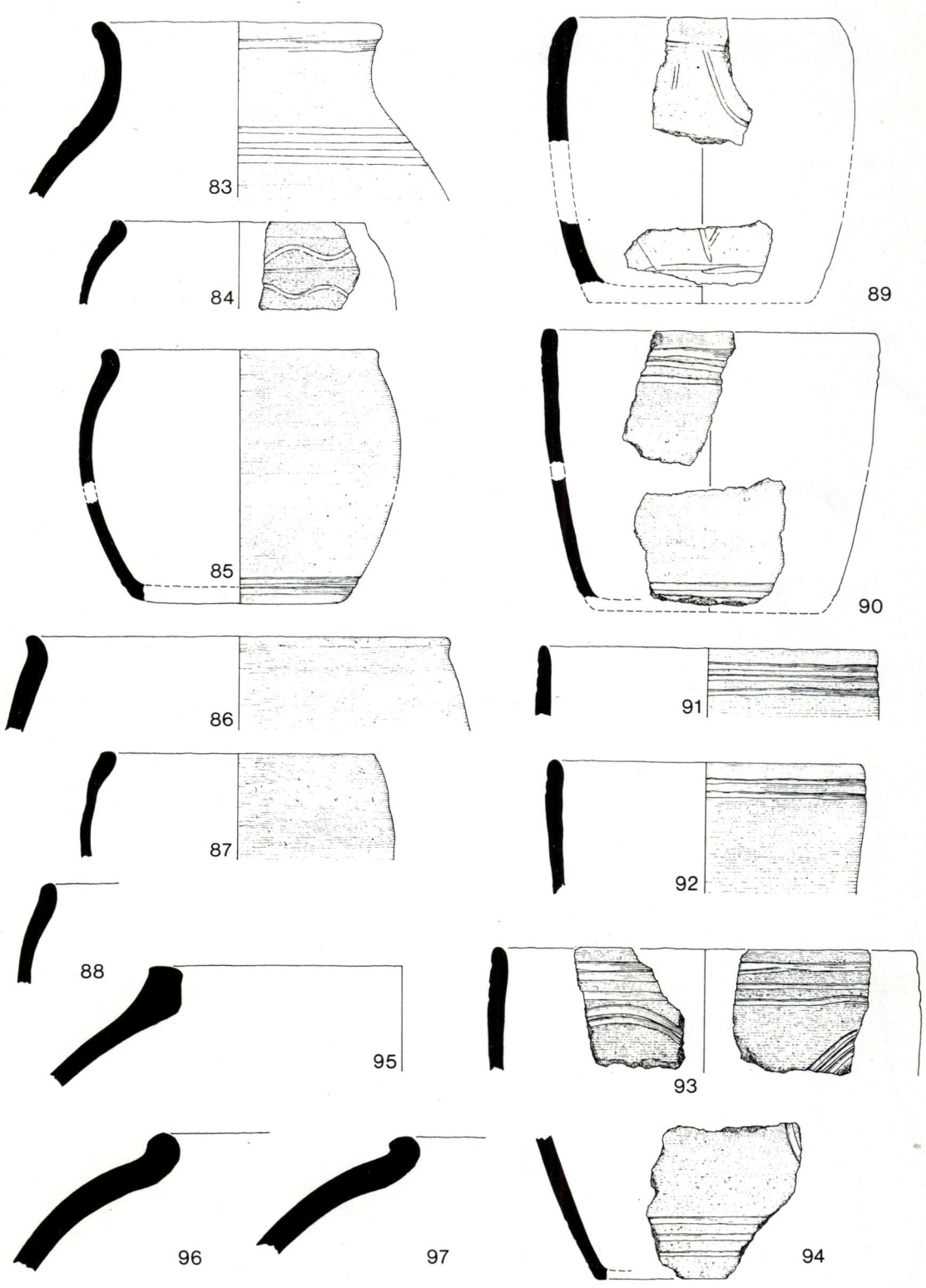

Fig. 20   Pottery: scale ¹/₃. Nos. 83–97, group 7 from posthole 9 at east gate
Fabrics: fabric C, Nos. 95–7; fabric E, Nos. 83–94

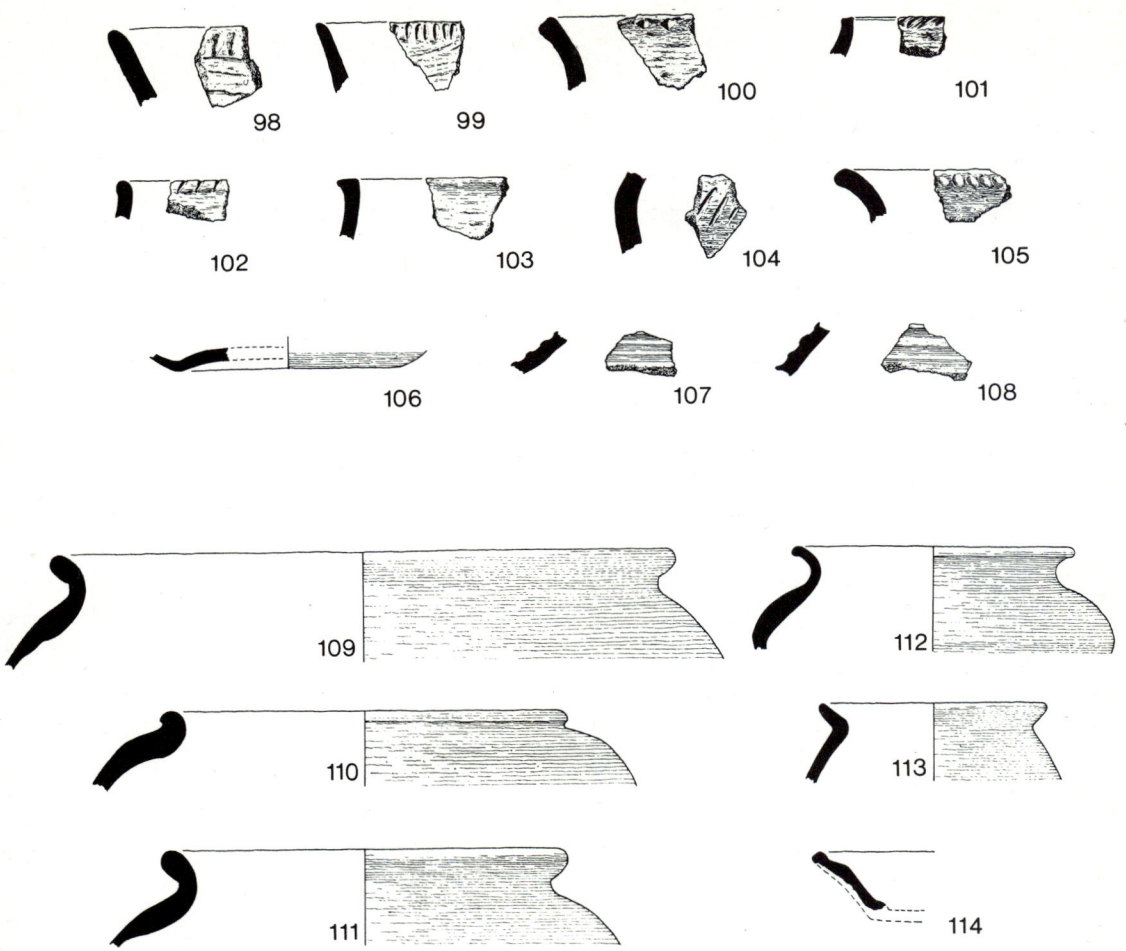

Fig.21   Pottery: scale $^1/_3$. Nos. 98–108, group 8, miscellaneous unstratified; Nos. 109–114, group 9, late pre-Roman Iron Age Fabrics: fabric A, No. 99; fabric B, Nos. 98, 100–5; fabric D, Nos. 106–8; fabric G, Nos. 109–114

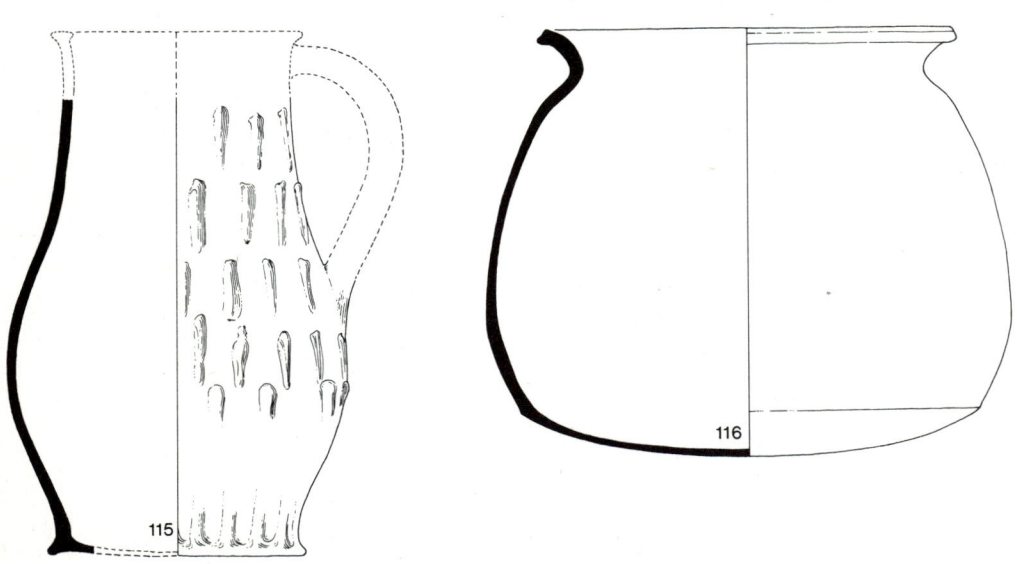

Fig.22   Pottery: scale $^1/_4$. Nos. 115–6, group 10, medieval vessels from field-boundary gully Fabrics: see p.19

Inner (original) entrance

Silt in south ditch end	A layer 4	Body sherds 1 fA; 1 fB
Gate post	F layer 5	Body sherd 1 fB
Silt in north end	E layer 3	Atrebatic or Roman sherds.
	E layer 4	Drawn, nos 43–65 186 fE; 37 fE; 4 fB.
	E layer 5	Body sherds 2 fA; 1fB
	E layer 7	Drawn, no.3 Body sherds 2 fE

Junction of cross-ditch and main fort ditch

Trench D	layer 4 (gully)	Body sherds, 3 fB
	layer 8 (rampart)	Body sherds, 2 fB
	layer 9 (cross-ditch fill)	Drawn, no.8 Body sherds 5 fB; 2 fD; 2 fE
	layer 10 (main fort ditch)	Body sherds 3 fA
	layer 11 (main fort ditch)	Drawn, no.9 Body sherds 4 fA; 4 fB; 4 fD; 6 fE
	layer 12 (rectangular gully)	Body sherd 1 fA
Trench G	layer 8 (rectangular gully)	Drawn, nos.10–18 Body sherds 7 fA; 36 fB; 2 fD; 15 fE; 2 fF
	layer 9 (cross-ditch fill)	Drawn, no.7 Body sherds 2 fA; 13 fB; 3 fD; 8 fE; 3 fE
	layers of rampart, layers 7, 10, 11, 12; derived, layer 2	Drawn, nos.19–34 (and 35–42 derived) Body sherds 4 fA; 45 fB; 20 fE; 4 fF
	layer 19 (main ditch fill)	Body sherds 12 fB; 7 fE; 1 fF

East entrance

South ditch end		Only sherds were discovered mainly in fB and fE which it is now difficult to relate to the section. The quantity was small.
North ditch end	CV layer 4	Drawn, nos.72–82 Body sherds 3 fE; 71 fE
	DIV layers 4 & 5	Body sherds 14 fE
	DVI layer 6	Body sherds 6 fC; 13 fE; 29 fB
Ditch C	A VIII layer 3	Body sherds 19 fG; (ie Atrebatic or early Roman)
	layer 6	Body sherds 6 fB
Ditch E	FIX layer 3	Body sherds 5 fA; 5 fB
Gate post 9 fill	BIII layers 8 & 9	Body sherds 11 fC; 5 fE
	occupation adjacent layer 5	Body sherds 22 fE (including 2 saucepan pot rims)
Gate post 10 fill	AIII layers, 4, 12, 13	Drawn, nos.83–97 Body sherds 26 fC; 82 fE; 3 fF
	occupation adjacent layer 5	Body sherds 15 fC; 6 fE
From layers of tumbled stones on road surface		Small quantity of abraded sherds in fabrics B and E. None in Atrebatic or Roman wares.

From the hollow way outside the fort in soil above the road surface	BIX layer 2	Drawn, nos.66–71 Body sherds 18 fE
From ploughsoil		Since the ploughsoil was deposited in the medieval period as the result of the constant scouring of the inside of the fort, it is only to be expected that quantities of abraded Iron Age pottery were found in it. Of the rims and decorated sherds, sherds 98–106 were selected for illustration: a few rims of saucepan pots and contemporary proto-bead-rim bowls were also recorded, but have not been illustrated. The ploughsoil in trench B′VIII, overlying the fill of ditch C, contained a quantity of late Atrebatic–early Roman ware, a selection of which is illustrated as 109–113. Sherds of this type were elsewhere rare. Later Roman pottery was represented by the base of a New Forest beaker from trench A′VIII and a few scraps from general ploughsoil layers.

Discussion

The earliest distinctive pottery from Torberry can, on typological grounds, be assigned to the early part of the pre-Roman Iron Age. It consists of the coarse ware jars (Nos 6, 98–105) with finger-tip or finger-nail decoration on the lip and shoulder. The general category to which these vessels belong is widely distributed in southern Britain, and is commonly found in an assemblage which has been called the Kimmeridge–Caburn style (Cunliffe 1974b, 33–4) dating broadly to the 6th century BC, but probably beginning earlier. This particular type, however, continued in use into the 5th century BC. The distinctive bipartite bowls which characterize the style have not yet been found at Torberry, but a sherd from the rim of a bowl with an outflared rim was recovered from the rampart of the cross-defence (No. 1) and an omphalos base, probably from a similar bowl, was found in the ploughsoil (No. 106). These bowls and two furrowed sherds (Nos. 107 and 108) found by Brightwell are related to hematite-coated vessels found commonly in Wessex in the 5th century and perhaps a little later. The rim sherd from the rampart was either dropped at the time of the construction of the first defence or was already lying about on the surface. Thus all that can safely be said of this typologically early group is that it indicates occupation on the hilltop in the 6th or 5th century, possibly before the defences were erected. If the absence of angular bipartite bowls is significant (and the sample is too small to be sure) the available evidence would favour a 5th rather than a 6th century origin for the occupation.

The early occupation of sites, later to become strongly defended hillforts, is well attested in the area, both at Trundle, Sussex (Curwen 1929, 1931), and at St Catherine's Hill, Hants (Hawkes, Myres, and Stevens 1930). The neighbouring hill fort at Harting Beacon, Sussex, is also said to have produced early pottery (Keef 1953).

The earliest closely stratified pottery from Torberry are the sherds (Nos. 3–5) from the lower silt of the recut cross-ditch. Of these the only distinctive feature is the low pedestal base (No. 3), which would not be out of place in a 4th or 3rd century context. Close dating on such slight evidence is, however, inadvisable.

The third-period rampart constructed over the partially silted cross-ditch, using turf and soil probably derived from inside the fort, provides a useful, well stratified group of material (Nos. 19–34), to which the sherds from the silt (Nos. 35–42) can probably be added. The coarse-ware jar tradition is still represented (Nos. 26, 27) but without the decoration which is typical of the earlier period. Most of the jars, however, were now made in a finer fabric with smoothed, usually dark fired surfaces, and with vestigial or rounded shoulders and often out-turned proto-bead-rims. Several of the vessels (eg Nos. 23, 28, 32) were simple open bowls with wide mouths. There can be little doubt that this group, both stratigraphically and typologically, precedes the development of the full 'saucepan pot' assemblage to be described below. It is essentially transitional between the old styles of the early pre-Roman Iron Age and the saucepan pot assemblage. The forms and fabrics are close to the saucepan pot types, but lack any decorative features, while the surface finish has not yet reached the highly burnished appearance typical of the later groups.

Compared to the Chalton site 50 vessels (pp. 37 ff), the Torberry group should be later, since its characteristics are far closer to the saucepan pot styles and it lacks the predominance of coarse shouldered jars and small bowls with flaring rims, which occur at Chalton site 50. Between them the two groups provide a valuable insight into the ceramic development of the area in the middle centuries of the pre-Roman Iron Age. Accurate dating is impossible, but the absence of distinctive 4th century types at Chalton would indicate a date late in the 4th or early in the 3rd century, with the Torberry assemblage following in the second half of the 3rd or even early 2nd century. While these approximations may be a good half-century out, they are the best that can be offered at the moment.

With the extension of the fort in phase 3, the cross-ditch ceased to serve a defensive function, and was allowed to silt up. In the ditch end on the north side of the now-abandoned entrance a quantity of occupation debris accumulated, including a substantial collection of pottery (Nos. 43–65). The group can be regarded as a closed assemblage belonging to the St Catherine's Hill–Worthy Down style of the saucepan pot continuum (Cunliffe 1964, 2–6; 1974a, 42–3). The group provides a full range of saucepan pot forms, from the slightly barrel-shaped types (eg No. 44) to those more like a flower pot (eg No. 49). Small plain bowls (Nos. 57–9), bowls with internally thickened rims (eg No. 62), and large proto-bead-rimmed jars (Nos. 55, 56) complete the assemblage. All were finely finished with smoothed and often highly burnished surfaces.

Shallow tooled decoration, executed while the fabric was leather-hard, is another distinctive characteristic. All the 'saucepans' were decorated in some form, usually with shallow tooled horizontal lines just below the rim or above the base angle. More elaborate arrangements include diagonal lines between rows of dots (No. 44) and wavy lines either flattened (Nos. 45, 46) or steeper (Nos. 43, 47?, 55). No. 43, with its band of short dashes between horizontal lines is yet another variant.

The decorative style of No. 44 is diagnostic of the St. Catherine's Hill–Worthy Down style, occurring in a broad zone from West Sussex right across Hampshire to the Downs west of the river Test. It is particularly common among the contemporary groups from Danebury, Hants. Within this extensive region, local preferences in decoration can be traced. The wavy lines for example, which occur at Torberry and at the Trundle (Curwen, 1929, pls. XII, XIII)

are more common at the eastern end of the region, while zones of oblique lines drawn in alternate directions predominate at the western end. Minor stylistic variations are only to be expected over so large an area.

Three other groups belonging to the saucepan pot tradition have been found at Torberry. Group 6 (Nos. 72–82) is either contemporary with, or a little later than, group 4. The same forms are represented, but with decorative variations. The remaining two groups, group 5 (Nos. 66–72) and group 7 (Nos. 83–94), should be stratigraphically later than groups 4 and 6, since they came from contexts immediately post-dating the abandonment of the east entrance – group 5 from above the roadway and group 7 from within the gate postholes. Although the groups are reasonably large, it is difficult to be sure that such differences as appear are chronologically significant. However, the large bead-rimmed storage jars (Nos. 95–97) and the necked jar (No. 83) do not occur in the earlier groups 4 and 6, while the later bowl forms (Nos. 70, 84, 85) appear to be rather more tightly moulded. Since all these characteristics recur in later assemblages of the southern Atrebatic style, they may tentatively be suggested to be diagnostic of a slightly later phase in the saucepan pot continuum. The problem of chronological variations is discussed again below (pp. 46–7), where the saucepan pot groups from Chalton site 15 are described.

The dating of the saucepan pot styles cannot be attempted with any pretensions of accuracy. Most of the developments described above probably belong within the 2nd century. By the middle of the 1st century, or soon after, the appearance of wheel-made types gave rise to the distinctive southern Atrebatic style. How long into the first half of the 1st century saucepan pot styles continued is a debatable matter, but if the arguments offered below (p. 46) in relation to Chalton site 15 pottery are accepted. the latest groups from Torberry are unlikely to date much after 100 BC.

Of the later pottery there is little to be said. Group 8 is typical of the pottery of the middle of the 1st century AD, though it is difficult to say whether it pre-dates or just post-dates the Roman conquest. Apart from two abraded sherds, nothing was found of the later Roman period. The two medieval vessels from the gully cut into the cross-bank (Group 9) provide interesting confirmation of the late medieval agricultural activity to which the hill was subjected.

THE ANIMAL BONES

The animal bones were identified by the present writer in 1960 under the guidance of Mr Eric Higgs of the Department of Archaeology, University of Cambridge. As might be expected from the nature of the layers excavated, the bones were few and fragmentary. In all some 266 fragments were identified, belonging to sheep/goat, pig, cow, horse, fallow deer, red deer, and dog. With so small a sample detailed statistics are of little value, but certain gross figures can be offered.

Site 1 (East entrance)

	No. of fragments	Min. no. of individuals	% based on min. no.	% based on no. of frags.
Sheep	40	9	56	66
Pig	9	3	19	15
Cow	11	3	19	18
Horse	1	1	6	1

Site 2 (Cross-ditch area)

	No. of fragments	Min. no. of individuals	% based on min. no.	% based on no. of frags.
Sheep	73	6	32	36
Pig	76	6	32	37
Cow	48	3	16	23
Horse	1	1	5	0.5
Dog	3	1	5	1.5
Red deer	3	1	5	1.5
Fallow deer	1	1	5	0.5

Since the sample from Site 2 tends to reflect the early phase of occupation, while that from Site 1 belongs almost exclusively to the later phase, the apparent differences in percentage might be thought to be of chronological significance, there being far greater reliance on sheep in the later period. With such a small sample, however, generalizations of this kind are unrealistic. For the same reason, no comment is offered on butchery or age variations.

SUMMARY OF THE STRUCTURAL SEQUENCE

The main phases in the sequence of land use on Torberry Hill may be summarized as follows:

Phase	Inner entrance	Junction area		East entrance
0	–	–	⎫	
1	original entrance	original cross-ditch		ditches E & F
2	replaced gate	recut cross-ditch	⎫	
3	abandoned: occupation rubbish	new south fort ditch	Rectangular Gully	original entrance and ditch D
4	–	–		inturned entrance and ditch C
5	–	–		destruction
6	–	–	⎭	Roman ploughing
7	medieval field boundary	ploughing		ploughing

Phase 0

Phase 0 has been created to allow for the possibility that the two ditches at the east entrance, ditches E and F, pre-date the construction of the cross-ditch. Since they are stratigraphically isolated and have produced only abraded body sherds of undatable coarse ware, they cannot be related to the main hillfort sequence except that ditch F pre-dates the roadway leading to the phase 3 entrance. Nor is there any reason to suppose that the two ditches are of the same date. Thus, while they may well be part of an enclosure related to the fort in phases 1 or 2, or even some kind of marking-out ditches for the phase 3 extension, they could equally possibly pre-date the construction of the fort.

Phase 1

The original defensive work of phase 1 consisted of a ditch, backed by a timber-faced (possibly box-constructed) rampart, built across the neck of the hill. The entire earthwork was less than 300 ft long and was pierced by a single entrance placed close to the scarp edge on the northern side of the ridge.

Phase 2

In phase 2 the entrance was slightly modified and the gate-posts reset. It was in this phase that the cross-ditch was re-cut and some of the rampart timbers were replaced. At the south end, the recent ditch diverged from the original line, leaving the original ditch end isolated to silt up. In all probability the divergence was caused by the fact that the defences were now taken around the western end of the hill to create a completely enclosed hillfort of 3½ acres (1.4 ha).

Phase 3

In phase 3 the enclosed area was extended to take in a further 2½ acres (1 ha) in front of the cross-defence, which was now slighted, the gate-posts being removed and the ditch partly filled with chalk rubble. Where the new defensive line joined the south-east corner of the original enclosure, a new ditch was dug across the filling of the old and a rampart, faced with turves, was constructed across the hollow of the old partially silted ditch.

The entrance was now sited at the east end of the new enclosure. The road ran diagonally between slightly overlapping ditch ends and was flanked by a short length of ditch (ditch D). Little is known of the form of the contemporary gate except that large postholes were dug on line with the ditch ends.

Phase 4

Later the gate was drastically modified. Blocking walls were constructed across the ditch ends, which were filled in order to accommodate a re-aligned roadway flanked by two substantial stone-built walls. The effect was to create a long inturned corridor, at the head of which was a massive timber gate. A short length of ditch (ditch C) was dug to protect the approach to one of the flanking walls.

Phase 5

Phase 5 represents the destruction of the east gate. The gate-posts were pulled out and the wall was thrown down to block the roadway.

Phase 6

A small group of mid-1st century AD pottery was found in the upper silting of ditch C. Roman sherds also occurred in the uppermost levels of the cross-ditch. The nature of this activity is uncertain, but it is not impossible that the hill began to be ploughed in the Roman period.

The 'rectangular gully' discovered in trenches D and G on site 2 is undated: all that can be said is that it belongs to the period covered by phases 2–6; but since it contains only Iron Age pottery it may belong to phases 2–4.

Phase 7

The documentary evidence shows that the hill must have been common pasture in 1399, for in that year fines were recorded for the trespass of 737 sheep. By the reign of Philip and Mary, however, it had been converted to arable land, and on a map of 1632 the hill is shown divided into a number of enclosures (Yates 1972, 33). Evidence of late medieval ploughing is extensive, both in the form of thick layers of ploughsoil filling the ditches and as lynchets which still survive on various parts of the site. A gully cut into the crest of the cross-bank, which contained medieval pottery dating to the late 14th or early 15th century, may belong to the original phase of medieval land clearance.

Since the 17th century the hill has been ploughed sproadically in times of national crisis but has, for the most part, remained as downland pasture. At the time of writing (May 1974) the hill has reverted to downland and is now once more cropped by a flock of Southdown sheep.

Dating of the phases

The assessment of the date of each phase is based partly on evidence of sequence and partly on the dates argued for the associated pottery discussed above. It should be stressed that these dates are only very approximate and represent the best that can be offered on available data.

Phase 0, which takes into account the pre-hillfort occupation, possibly including ditches E and F, might reasonably be assigned to the 6th century on the basis of a few unstratified sherds.

Phase 1 is later than the appearance of this type of pottery and incorporates a bowl sherd to which a 5th century date is appropriate.

Phase 2 which represents the clearing out of the cross-ditch, is best assigned to the 5th–4th centuries, since a sherd of that date range or a little later was found in the lower silt of the ditch.

Phase 3 represents an enlargement taking place at the time when pottery of the 3rd–early–2nd century was in use.

Phase 4 The occupation of both phases 3 and 4 was associated with saucepan pots assigned to the 2nd century.

Phase 5 The destruction of the gate took place while saucepan pots were still in use, possibly about 100 BC.

Phase 6 merely represents sporadic use in the 1st–4th centuries AD.

Phase 7 is dated on documentary evidence to the 15th or 16th centuries. The pottery favours an early 15th century date.

STRUCTURAL COMPARISONS

In its latest phase, Torberry belongs to a well known class of 'contour' hillforts which are widely distributed in Britain, particularly in the south and west of the country, extending in a broad arc from Sussex to the Welsh borderland. Many structural details are shared in common between these forts, and it is possible to distinguish certain directional trends in their development. The broader issues have been considered elsewhere (Cunliffe 1974a, 227–263). Here it is necessary to compare Torberry only with its more immediate neighbours in Sussex and Hampshire.

The earliest phase of the Torberry defences, the cross-bank and ditch with its early entrance (phase 1), appears, from the evidence in trench B, to have incorporated a timber box-structured rampart with vertical timbers both front and rear, presumably cross-braced with horizontal members. Such a structure is typical of the Hollingbury style of timber strengthening named after the type-site excavated in 1931 (Curwen 1932, figs. 1 and 2), for which a date in the early pre-Roman Iron Age is accepted. Normally earthworks of this kind were provided with a berm between the external timber facing of the rampart and the lip of the ditch, a feature which the Torberry cross-defence displays, even though the ditch itself is likely to have been recut.

The problem of whether or not the defences were extended around the west end of the hill in phase 2 has already been discussed (p. 6). The single section across this line (trench X) produced evidence of only a front timber revetment at this point, an observation which, if substantiated, would be consistent with a phase 2 or 3 date, since it appears that deeply bedded rear timbering was eventually abandoned in southern Britain towards the middle of the pre-Roman Iron Age (Cunliffe 1974a, 231–2).

The inner gate in both its phases was a single portal structure aligned approximately with the crest of the rampart or a little in front of it. The obvious comparisons are with Hollingbury (Curwen 1932, fig.2) and Danebury in its first phase (Cunliffe 1971b, fig.7). Danebury even has fence trenches flanking the ditch ends which are closely comparable with Torberry. Comparison can also be made with the gate at Quarley Hill (Hawkes 1939, fig.12), where at least two phases tend to complicate the picture. In one phase, however, massive elongated post pits defined a simple gate, set back a little behind the rampart crest. All the above structures can with reasonable certainty be assigned to the period centring on the 5th and 4th centuries, a date acceptable but not proven for the Torberry inner gate.

The next stage in local gate construction, exemplified by St Catherine's Hill phase 1, Danebury phase 2a, and Trundle phase 2 (summarized in Cunliffe 1974a, fig.13.7), involved the creation of a dual portal entrance with recesses behind. Such a structure does not appear to occur at Torberry unless it is the little known outer entrance of phase 3.

In its first defended phase, Torberry was a promontory fort, created by the construction of a single cross-dyke which effectively defined the western end of the hill. That this was so was discovered only as the result of excavation and could not have been demonstrated by field survey alone. The discovery raises the interesting question of how many other forts may have originated in this way. Such an origin is possible for Hammer Wood, Sussex (Boyden 1958), and may even prove to be true for Old Winchester Hill, Hants., where the earthwork that crosses the neck of land at the east end of the ridge is more massive than the others and is rather awkwardly attached to the earthworks constituting the rest of the circuit. Only excavation will solve the problem.

The extension of the hillfort to the east increased the enclosed area from 3½ acres (1.4 ha) to 6 acres (2.4 ha), and brought Torberry into line with the style of contour defences displayed by its neighbours, St Catherine's Hill, Hants., Old Winchester Hill, Hants., and The Trundle, Sussex. The form of the original main gate (phase 3) has not been recovered, but the two holes at the ditch ends pose interesting problems (pp. 9–10), and can only be paralleled by the reported situation at Glyne, Sussex (Burstow, pers. comm.).

The rebuilt gate of period 4 is, however, a monumental example of a well known type which has a widespread distribution at the end of the 2nd and beginning of the 1st century BC in Britain (Cunliffe 1974a, 243–50) and on the continent (Wheeler and Richardson, 1957, e.g. pl. IV and XX; Dehn 1961). The overriding desire seems to have been to create a long corridor-like approach in advance of a narrow but massive gate. At Torberry this was effected in grand style by building a pair of flanking walls defining a passage 85 ft (26 m) long. Several other local examples

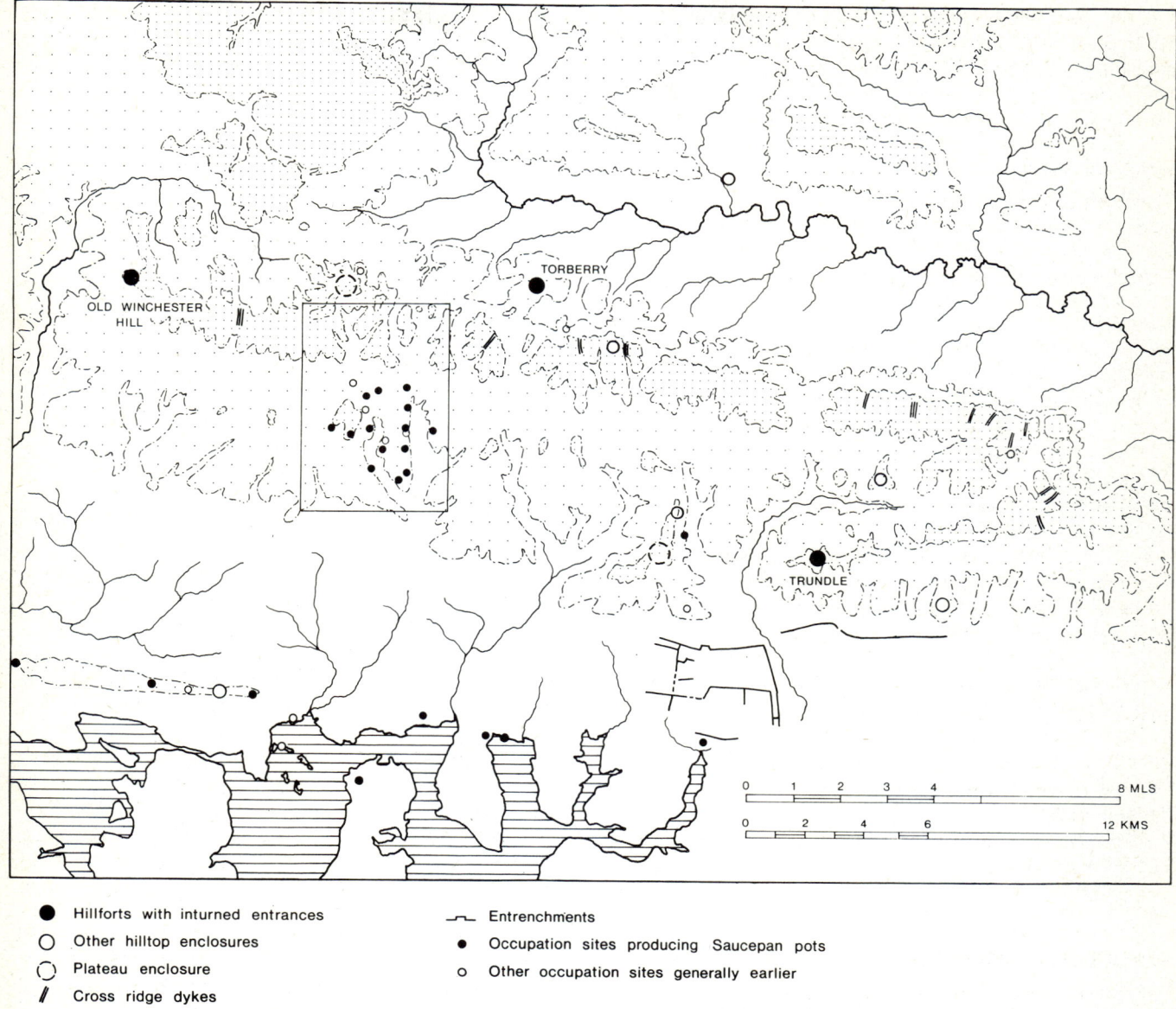

●	Hillforts with inturned entrances
○	Other hilltop enclosures
◌	Plateau enclosure
∕	Cross ridge dykes

⌐	Entrenchments
•	Occupation sites producing Saucepan pots
○	Other occupation sites generally earlier

Fig.23   First millennium BC settlement on the South Downs. The area intensively surveyed in the vicinity of Chalton is outlined [North at top]

have been excavated. In the last phase of The Trundle (Curwen 1931, pl.V) a double gate was set at the end of a corridor 60 ft (c. 18 m) long flanked by flint-built walls, while at St Catherine's Hill the inturned effect was created by the modification of the existing wide entrance, giving rise to a corridor 55 ft long (c. 17 m), at least partly lined with flint walls (Cunliffe 1974a, fig. 13.10). Buckland Rings, near Lymington, Hants. (Hawkes 1936, fig.6), provides an interesting variant in which a turf-walled corridor 85 ft (26 m) long was increased in effective length by means of a second line of rampart and ditch outside the main ditch. Danebury, Hants., on the other hand, makes use of outworks to extend the corridor to a length of 147 ft (45 m) (Cunliffe 1971b, figs. 6 and 7). Further west, in Wiltshire and Dorset, complex outworks become the norm (for comparative plans, Cunliffe 1974a, fig. 13.11).

It may be said, therefore, that the Torberry phase 4 entrance lies firmly within a broad tradition of defensive

architecture which in most of Hampshire and Sussex marks the last phase of hillfort development. It is only in the west from Dorset to the Welsh border area that further stages of elaboration can be traced extending throughout the 1st century BC into the 1st century AD.

THE PHYSICAL AND CULTURAL ENVIRONMENT (Fig.23)

Torberry is one of three locations between the rivers Meon and Arun to have developed into a strongly defended hillfort by the 3rd and 2nd centuries BC. Its neighbours are Old Winchester Hill, situated some 8 miles (13 km) to the west, and The Trundle, lying at about the same distance to the south-east. All three sites share physical characteristics in common; they are all contour forts, all have long inturned entrances, and all lie within about 1 mile (1.6 km) of permanent water supplies. The dating evidence from Torberry and The Trundle suggests contemporaneity; Old Winchester

Hill is unexcavated but is so like the others that all three may reasonably be regarded as having been in use at the same time. Thus each hillfort is likely to have been the 'centre-place' for a considerable territory, the exact size and shape of which is beyond discovery. Assuming that the sites were of equal importance, the political territory of Torberry might tentatively be thought to extend for at least 4 miles in each direction, and could well have reached even further north into the Weald and south across the Downs to the coastal plain. The absence of natural or artificial boundaries makes precise definition impossible.

Torberry evidently commanded a rich variety of resource potentials. In the immediate vicinity lay the fertile calcareous soils of the Upper Greensand, which form a bench a mile or so (c. 1.6 km) wide at the foot of the South Down scarp. This environment was extensively exploited in Roman times and later, in the Saxon period, saw the development of closely spaced villages clearly reflecting its favourable qualities for settlement and food production. To the north lay the Weald, providing extensive areas of dense woodland on the bands of clay, interspersed with lighter sandy soils which may at this time already have developed into heathland. Such an environment could have provided unlimited supplies of timber and building stone, of the kind used in the construction of the east entrance, together with well watered pannage for swine and cattle. In addition, a wide range of woodland products such as herbs, dyes, and relishes, as well as game would have been readily available. To the south lay the chalk Downs, which at this time were densely occupied by farming communities, as the survey of the Chalton area shows (Cunliffe 1974b). The downlands would have been the principal area for the production of grain and sheep. The lack of readily available water would have rendered large-scale cattle rearing hazardous.

Whatever the military implications of these late hillforts might be, there can be little reasonable doubt that they served a significant economic function as redistribution centres for the products of their hinterlands. It is possible that through such centres, by long-distance trade and exchange, luxury objects such as shale bracelets and glass beads were introduced into the area. The precise functions of these hillforts cannot, of course, be determined until at least one of them has been totally excavated.

The general settlement pattern of the 3rd and 2nd centuries BC is reasonably well known, the range of occupation sites consisting of small farmsteads and strongly defended hillforts of Old Winchester—Torberry—Trundle type. Before that, in the early centuries of the pre-Roman Iron Age, the situation is more obscure. Settlement at Torberry and The Trundle goes back to at least the 6th or 5th century, but there is no positive evidence of defences at this date. There is, however, one hilltop enclosure which may belong to this early period — Harting Beacon, situated on the crest of the Downs 2 miles (3 km) south-east of Torberry. The site was partially explored in the 1950's by Miss P A M Keef, who records the existence of two gold 'lock rings' and pottery of 'Iron Age A2 type' (Keef 1953). The 'lock rings' are, as Childe pointed out in Miss Keef's note, of Late Bronze Age type. He preferred to assign them to the Hallstatt B phase, but admitted that they could last into Hallstatt C, in other words a date range of c. 900—600 BC. If the 'A2' pottery is of the type we would now assign to the Kimmeridge—Caburn style (Cunliffe 1966), a date in the 7th or 6th

century is probable. Thus the gold and pottery could well overlap in date in the 7th century and suggest that the enclosure may have been in use at that time. The absence of later material would allow it to have been superseded by Torberry.

Two other enclosures of Iron Age date are known in the area: the promontory enclosure at Hammer Wood, Iping (Boyden 1958) and the hill-slope enclosure on Bow Hill known as Goosehill Camp (Boyden 1956). Both have been sampled by trial excavation, but dating is difficult with so little material available. At best all that can be said is that they are likely to belong to the middle part of the pre-Roman Iron Age, after the Kimmeridge—Caburn style but before the development of saucepan pots. Goosehill is clearly atypical and appears to have been little more than an enclosed farmstead, while Hammer Wood, though of hillfort proportions, was almost totally barren of finds. It therefore remains a possibility that it was never occupied but perhaps served a specialized function, such as providing safe kraal space for flocks and herds.

Two other types of substantial field monument are represented in the region: cross-ridge dykes and plateau enclosures, both of which are likely to pre-date the Iron Age and may well be of 2nd millennium date. The function and dating of cross-ridge dykes remains obscure but that they served as some kind of territorial division seems likely (Fowler 1964). The plateau enclosures, of which Butser Hill and Bow Hill are examples, are equally enigmatic. They appear to represent upland areas demarcated and partially enclosed possibly to serve as places of assembly (Cunliffe 1971a, 57; 1976). If so, they may be the successors of the Neolithic causewayed camp henge monument tradition.

It is suggested, then, that Torberry and its contemporary equals, Old Winchester Hill and The Trundle, may be seen as the end-product of a long period of social and economic development; they represent 'centre-places' serving a well defined hinterland in much the same way as the causewayed camp on The Trundle served the 3rd millennium communities and the plateau enclosures served those of the 2nd. The 1st millennium saw the introduction of increasingly strong defences (contrast Harting Beacon with Torberry) and the gradual appearance of what could be interpreted as a resident population. These broadly linked generalizations seem on present evidence to hold good for much of southern England.

ACKNOWLEDGMENTS

Had it not been for the indefatigable activities of Mr Brightwell, the hillfort of Torberry may well have remained undiscovered. His enquiring persistence and his willingness to share his results with others were instrumental in ensuring that the site received the attention from the archaeological world which it deserved. The instigation of the programme of excavation, which took place between 1956 and 1958, and its subsequent execution, was entirely due to the far-sighted efforts of Mr John Boyden, who created for the purpose a local excavation committee (the Joint Archaeological Committee), and worked unsparingly to see the project completed satisfactorily. The skill with which the excavation was directed by Dr G Duncan and the high quality of the site recording system have made the preparation of the descriptive part of this report a comparatively simple matter.

The excavations were carried out by kind permission of the then owner, Mr K Bawtry of Church Farm, South Harting, in whose possession the finds remain. The site records have been deposited in Chichester City Museum.

In preparing this report in May 1974, I would particularly like to record my thanks to John Boyden for the help he has given in so many ways. The drawings of the pottery and the small finds were prepared by Mr Mike Rouillard, while the publication prints from the original excavation negatives were produced by Mr R Wilkins. Mr Tim Ambrose kindly read the text and offered many helpful comments.

BIBLIOGRAPHY

Boyden, J R, 1956 'Excavations at Goosehill Camp 1953–5' *Sussex Archaeol Collect* **94** (1956), 70–99.

Boyden, J R, 1958 'Excavations at Hammer Wood, Iping; 1957' *ibid.,* **96** (1958), 149–63.

Bulleid, A, and Gray, H St G, 1911 *The Glastonbury Lake Village* Vol. 1 (Glastonbury Antiquarian Society 1911).

Bulleid, A, and Gray, H St G, 1917 *The Glastonbury Lake Village* Vol. 2 (Glastonbury Antiquarian Society 1917).

Calkin, J B, 1949 'The Isle of Purbeck in the Iron Age' *Proc. Dorset Natur. Hist. Archaeol. Soc.,* **70** (1949), 25–59.

Calkin, J B, 1953 'Kimmeridge coal-money' *ibid.,* **75** (1953), 45–71

Cunliffe, B W, 1964 *Winchester Excavations 1949–1960* Vol. 1 (Winchester 1964).

Cunliffe, B W, 1966 'Stoke Clump, Hollingbury and the Early pre-Roman Iron Age in Sussex' *Sussex Archaeol, Collect* **104** (1966), 109–20.

Cunliffe, B W, and Phillipson, D, 1968 'Excavations at Eldon's Seat, Encombe, Dorset' *Proc. Prehist. Soc.* **34** (1968), 191–237.

Cunliffe, B W, 1971a 'Some Aspects of Hillforts and their Cultural Environments', in Hill, D, and Jesson, M (eds). *The Iron Age and its Hill-forts* (Southampton), 53–70.

Cunliffe, B W, 1971b 'Danebury, Hampshire: First Interim Report on the Excavation, 1969–70' *Antiq. J.* **51** (1971), 240–52.

Cunliffe, B W, 1974a *Iron Age Communities in Britain* (London 1974).

Cunliffe, B W, 1974b 'Chalton, Hants: the Evolution of a Landscape' *Antiq. J.* **53** (1973), 173–90.

Cunliffe, B W, 1976 'Hill-forts and Oppida in Britain' in Longworth, I H, Sieveking, G de G, and Wilson K E, *Problems in Economic and Social Archaeology* (Cambridge), 343–58.

Curwen, E C, 1929 'Excavation in the Trundle, Goodwood, 1928', *Sussex Archaeol. Collect.* **70** (1929), 33–85.

Curwen, E C, 1931 'Excavations in the Trundle' *ibid.* **72** (1931), 100–50.

Curwen, E C, 1932 'Excavations at Hollingbury Camp, Sussex' *Antiq J* **12** (1932), 1–16.

Curwen, E C, 1954 *The Archaeology of Sussex,* 2nd ed, (London 1954).

Dehn, W, 1961 'Zangentore an spätkeltischen Oppida' *Pamatky Archaeologické* **52.2** (1961), 390.

Fowler, P J, 1964 'Cross Dykes on the Ebble-Nadder Ridge', *Wiltshire Archaeol Natur Hist Mag* **59** (1964), 46–57.

Hawkes, C F.C, Myres, J N L, and Stevens, C G, 1930 *St. Catherine's Hill, Winchester* (Winchester 1930).

Hawkes, C F C, 1936 'The Excavations at Buckland Rings, Lymington, 1935' *Proc. Hampshire Fld Club Archaeol Soc.* **13** (1936), 124–64.

Hawkes, C F C, 1939 'The excavations at Quarley Hill, 1938' *ibid.* (1939), 136–94.

Keef, P A M, 1953 'Two gold pennanular ornaments from Harting Beacon, Sussex' *Antiq J* **33** (1953), 204–6.

Richmond, I A, 1968 *Hod Hill, Vol. 2: Excavations Carried out between 1951 and 1958* (London 1968).

Ward-Perkins, J B, 1944 'Excavations at the Iron Age Hill Fort of Oldbury, near Ightham, Kent' *Archaeologia* **90** (1944), 127–76.

Wheeler, R E M, and Richardson, K M, 1957 *Hill Forts of Northern France* (London 1957).

Yates, E M, 1972 *A History of the Landscapes of the Parishes of South Harting and Rogate* (Chichester 1972).

Two Pre-Roman Iron Age Sites at Chalton, Hampshire

The extensive programme of area survey carried out in the vicinity of Chalton, Hants., close to the border with Sussex, has brought to light a large number of archaeological sites (Cunliffe 1974b) including nineteen which can be dated to the pre-Roman Iron Age (Fig.24). For the most part these sites were located by discovering pottery scatters exposed after ploughing, but two of them, sites 15 and 50, came to light during construction work and were partially excavated as part of a general rescue programme.

Both sites lie on ridges of chalk a little above 400 ft (122 m) OD on east-facing slopes, 1¼ miles (2 km) apart. Both have been extensively ploughed in recent years and are now represented only by pits and postholes, all earthwork features and superficial stratigraphy having been removed. They are, however, notable for the well stratified groups of pottery recovered.

SITE 50 (Figs.25 and 26)

Site 50 was discovered in September 1968 during contractors' work involved in the re-alignment of the A3, the main road from Portsmouth to London. Immediately the topsoil had been removed, Mrs J Chaplin and Mr J Budden, who were watching for archaeological material, recognized several pits, which were excavated within the following few days by Mr Budden and the writer. A careful search of the entire cleared strip showed that only six pits extended into the road zone. Seven postholes were also discovered, but the possibility remains that others of a more shallow nature may have disappeared in the mechanical stripping process which disturbed the surface of the natural chalk. Subsequent field walking suggests that the centre of the site lies to the east of the road in an area which remains undisturbed arable land.

Descriptions of the pits (Fig.26)

Pit 1

4 ft 6 in (1.37 m) in diameter, 3 ft 7 in (1.09 m) deep. The lowest fill, layer 4, consisted of a mass of black soil, charcoal, and burnt flints which appeared to have been thrown in immediately after the pit ceased to be used. Then followed the frost-shattering and erosion of the pit sides, giving rise to layer 3, before a further deposit of burnt flints, charcoal, and ash (layer 2) was thrown in. The hollow in the top of the pit was filled with grey-brown stony soil (layer 1) resulting from gradual silting.

Pit 2

4 ft (1.22 m) in diameter at the top, of bell shape, 4 ft 6 in (1.37 m) deep.

The lowest layer, layer 4, was of loose chalk rubble, some of the blocks measuring up to 5 in (0.13 m) long. Above this came a thickness of smaller chalk rubble (layer 3) in a matrix of brown loam with flecks of charcoal. Both these layers were probably the result of natural erosion and silting. Layer 2 consisted of a mass of burnt flints and charcoal deliberately thrown in and sealed by layer 1, which incorporated some large flints in a matrix of grey-brown soil.

Pit 3

4 ft (1.22 m) in diameter and 2 ft 7 in (0.79 m) deep.

Layer 3 consisted of a tip of black soil containing occupation rubbish and some lumps of chalk. It was sealed by orange-brown clayey soil (layer 2). The top of the pit was filled with dark brown to black soil intermixed with large flint nodules and some burnt flints (layer 1). All three layers appear to have been deliberate tips.

Pit 4

Roughly rectangular in plan, measuring 2 ft 6 in (0.76 m) wide by 5 ft (1.52 m) long: approximately 2 ft 9 in (0.84 m) deep.

The filling was uniform throughout, consisting of chalk rubble, some of the blocks measuring up to 5 in (0.13 m) long. In the top levels some soil had penetrated the spaces between the blocks. The top 1 ft 6 in (0.46 m) contained lumps of light cindery material. Since no Iron Age material was found in the pit and its form is atypical, it may not be of Iron Age date.

Pit 5

3 ft 6 in (1.07 m) in diameter, 1 ft 2 in (0.36 m) deep.

On the bottom of the pit was a thin layer of charcoal which was sealed by a mass of crumbled, cream-coloured daub (layer 2), mixed with occasional lumps of charcoal; some of the daub showed signs of having been burnt before deposition. Layer 1 consisted of brown loamy soil which probably resulted from natural processes of silting.

Pit 6

2 ft 9 in (0.84 m) in diameter, 1 ft 8 in (0.51 m) deep.

The lowest layer (layer 3) consisted of a fine grey-brown soil containing a few burnt flints. It was sealed by a discontinuous layer of fragmented daub (layer 2). Above this was a uniform filling of loosely packed brown soil mixed with charcoal and flints (layer 1). All layers appear to be the result of deliberate filling.

Description of the postholes

Posthole 1: 2 ft x 1 ft 8 in (0.61 x 0.51 m); 8 in (0.21 m) deep. Filled with grey-brown stony soil containing quantities of potsherds.
Postholes 2—7: averaging 9—12 in (0.23—0.30 m) in diameter by 6—9 in (0.15—0.23 m) deep. Filled with chalky soil; no finds.

General considerations

There is little to be said of the nature of the site. The quantity of occupation debris in the pits, however, suggests that the domestic activities, normally associated with an

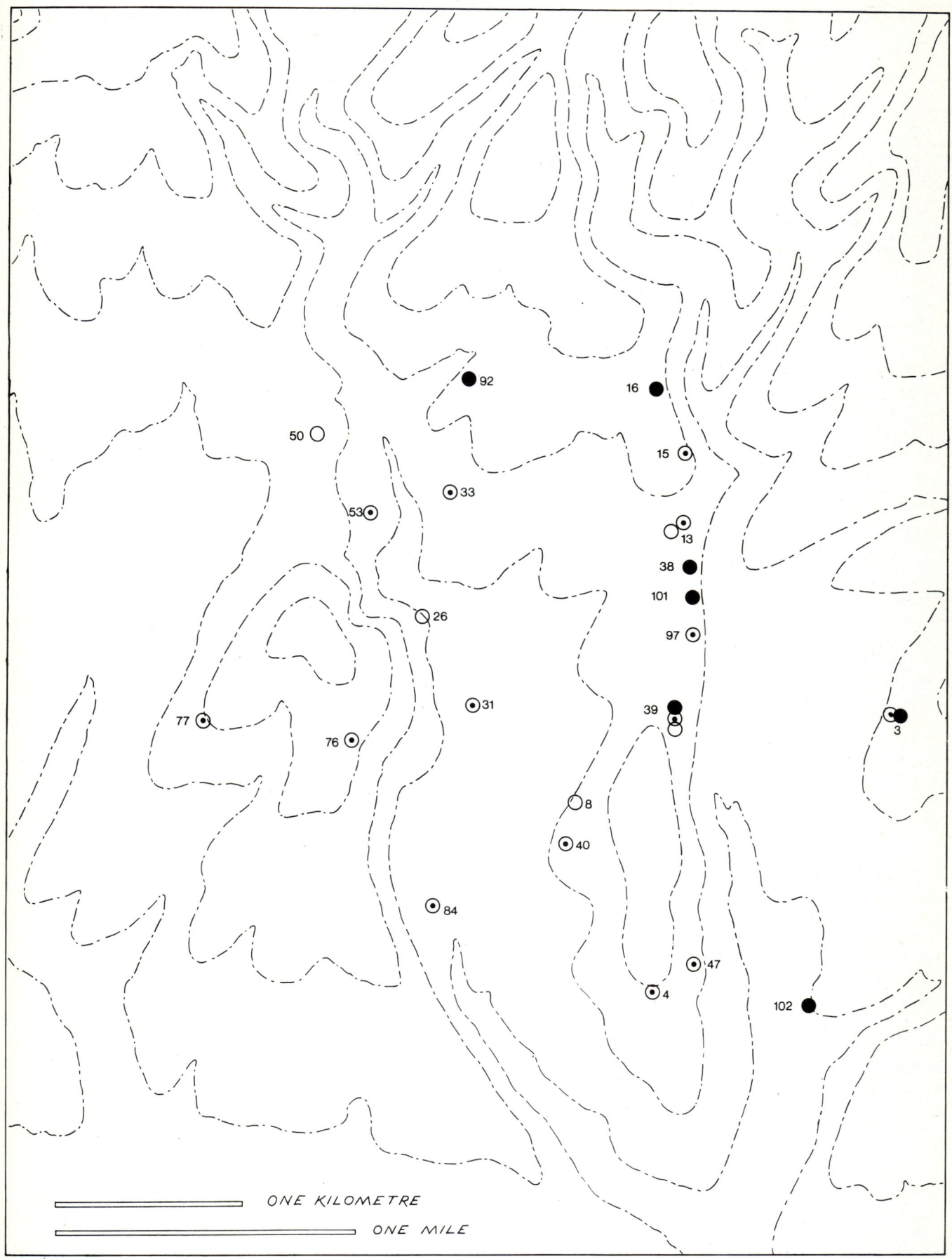

Fig. 24   General plan of Chalton area. Contours at intervals of
100 ft; highest contour 700 ft

ONE KILOMETRE

ONE MILE

SETTLEMENTS   ○ c 1000 – 400 B.C.

⊙ c 400 – 100 B.C.   ● c 100 – 0 B.C.

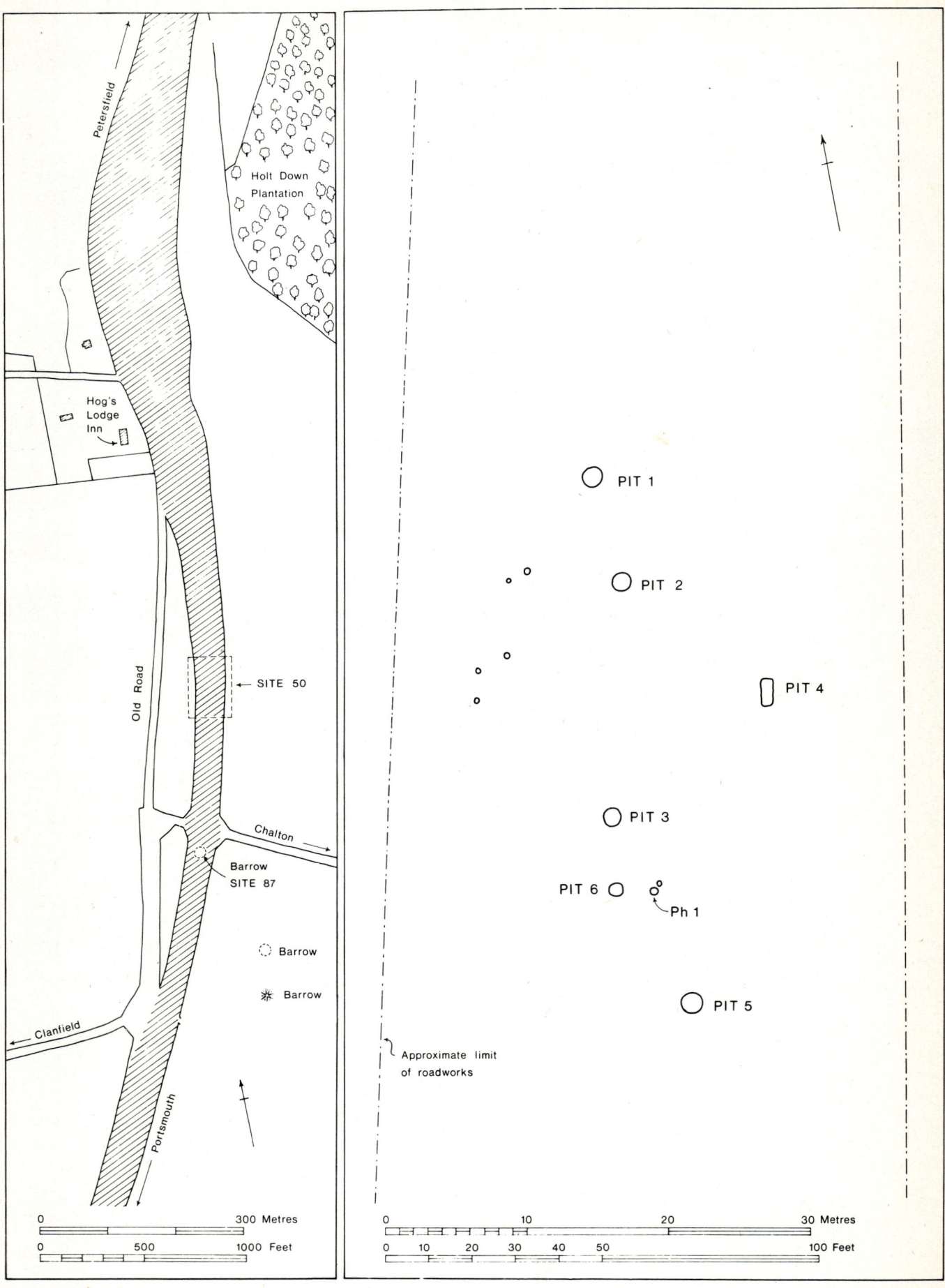

Petersfield

Holt Down
Plantation

Hog's
Lodge
Inn

Old Road

SITE 50

Chalton

Barrow
SITE 87

Barrow

Barrow

Clanfield

Portsmouth

0   300 Metres

0   500   1000 Feet

PIT 1

PIT 2

PIT 4

PIT 3

PIT 6   Ph 1

PIT 5

Approximate limit
of roadworks

0   10   20   30 Metres

0   10   20   30   40   50   100 Feet

Fig.25   Location plan for Chalton site 50 and site plan

PIT 1

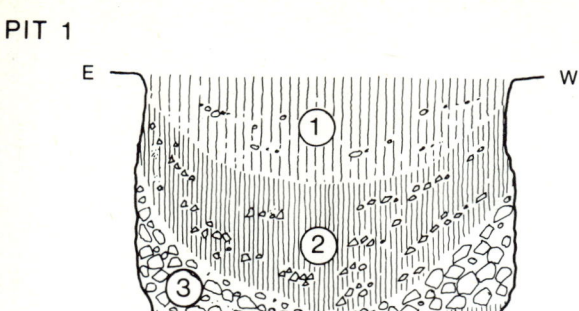

PIT 2

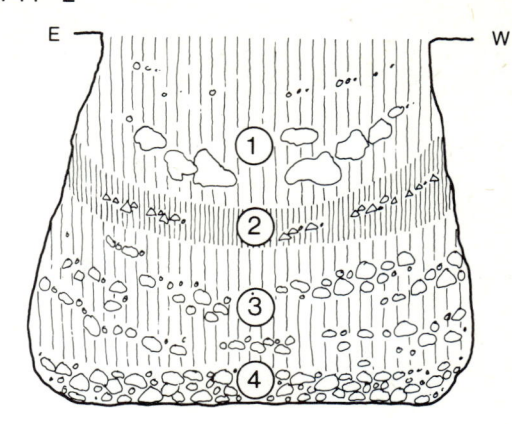

PIT 3

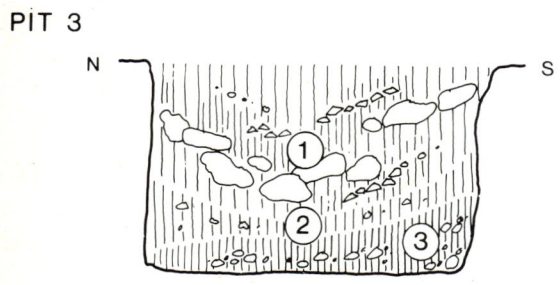

PIT 4

Section not drawn

PIT 5

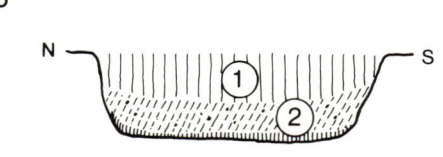

PIT 6

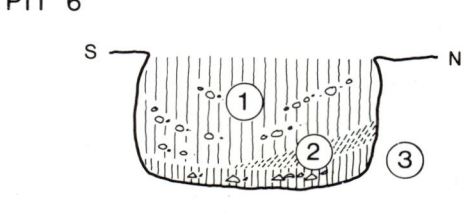

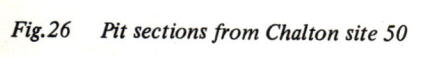

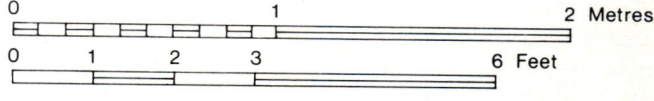

Fig.26   Pit sections from Chalton site 50

Iron Age farmstead, were being carried out nearby. Pottery was comparatively plentiful, and appears to have spanned only a short period of time (pp. 37ff.). Whether the entire settlement was as short-lived or not will only be decided if and when the rest of the area is examined.

SITE 15 (Figs.27 and 28)

Site 15 was discovered in August 1959 by Mr J Budden, while creating a hole in which to embed a fence post. Realizing that the mixed soil which he had disturbed was of archaeological interest, he called in Mr A Corney of Portsmouth City Museum, who carried out a limited ex-cavation, during the course of which two Iron Age pits (pits 1 and 2) were uncovered. By 1964 the fence had been re-moved and the enlarged field was being intensively culti-vated. In view of the destructive nature of the ploughing, it was decided to examine an area adjacent to the pits, after the mechanical stripping of the topsoil, in an attempt to determine the limits of the site. In effect only two more pits were found (pits 3 and 4), together with two pairs of

postholes. The natural chalk hereabouts was shattered and fissured and was being actively eroded to such an extent that it is unlikely that shallow features could have survived.

Description of the pits (Fig.28)

Pit 1

5 ft 3 in (1.60 m) in diameter, 3 ft 6 in (1.07 m) deep.

The lowest filling (layer 6) consisted of a fine loamy soil containing flecks of charcoal, which had probably washed into the pit after it had been abandoned. Then followed a period during which the sides of the pit eroded, resulting in a layer of shattered chalk (layer 5) heaped up around the pit walls. After this, a thick deposit of small chalk frag-ments and soil washed in (layer 4) presumably as the result of natural silting processes. Layer 3 which followed was a lens of clean yellow clay, possibly disintegrated daub, thrown in at the same time as fragments of burnt clay. This was sealed by dark grey soil (layer 2) containing a large greensand slab and lumps of chalk, together with three

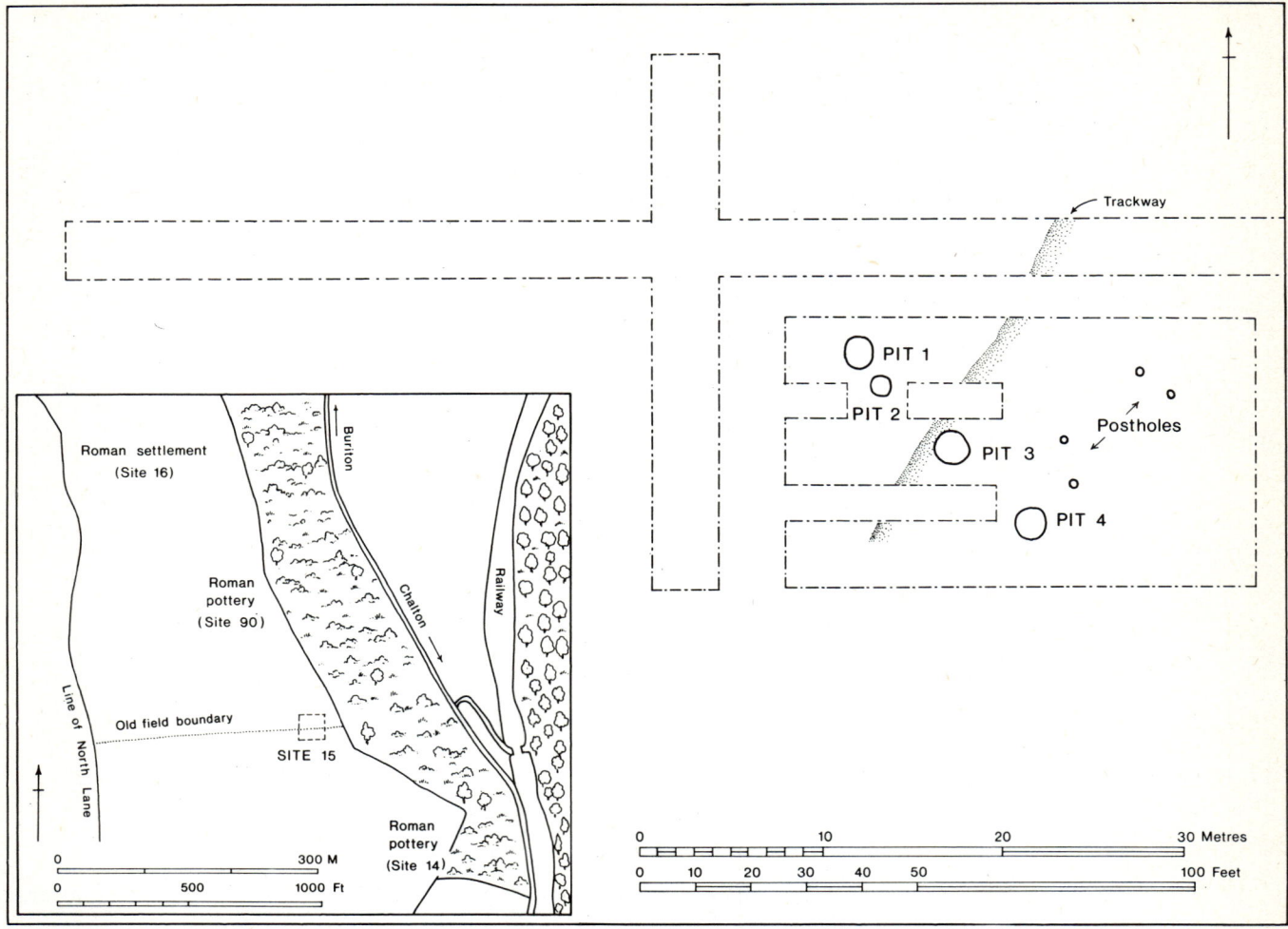

Fig.27   Location plan for Chalton site 15 and site plan

selected flint nodules, each perforated by a natural hole. The layer has the appearance of having been deliberately tipped in at one time. The hollow in the top of the pit was filled with a brown soil (layer 1), representing a natural soil accumulation.

Pit 2

3 ft (0.91 m) in diameter, 1 ft (0.31 m) deep.

The lowest layer (layer 2) was a discontinuous lens of sandy ash. This was sealed by a mass of black soil, charcoal, and burnt flints (layer 1).

Pit 3

6 ft (1.83 m) in diameter at the top where the side has eroded back, but only 3 ft 6 in (1.07 m) across at the bottom, 4 ft 6 in (1.37 m) deep.

The lowest layer (layer 10) consisted of large lumps of chalk derived from the shattered sides of the pit. Immediately above was a lens of decomposed chalky daub (layer 9), which was sealed by a layer of black soil mixed with charcoal and burnt flints (layer 8). Next came a layer of chalky rubble (layer 6), representing a further stage in the erosion of the pit sides. Some large blocks of chalk had become detached from the walls, but were embedded in the accumulating silt and fine chalk. In the hollow above this was a mass of greyish chalky soil (layer 5) containing pieces

of daub, and quantities of charcoal including a thick lens of charcoal at the base. Within this layer was a mass of chalk which had eroded from the east face of the pit (layer 7). The upper part of the pit was filled with an orange stony soil, possibly a ploughsoil of uncertain age (layer 4).

Pit 4

4½ ft (1.37 m) in diameter, 3 ft 3 in (0.99 m) deep.

The bottom of the pit was covered by a layer of brown soil (layer 7), which must have washed in when the pit was open. Above was a mass of loose chalk rubble (layer 6) derived from the weathering of the pit sides, which merged into the rather more marly layer 5. The surface of this layer appears to have been trampled hard. Thereafter more shattered chalk from the pit sides fell in (layer 4), followed by the deliberate deposition of a thick layer of black soil, charcoal and burnt flints (layer 3). The top of the pit was packed with large flints mixed with brown soil (layer 2), presumably deliberately thrown in.

The postholes

Four postholes were found, all averaging 9–12 in (0.23–0.31 m) in diameter and between 10 and 18 in (0.25–0.46 m) deep. They formed two pairs, similar to those generally considered to belong to racks or frames possibly for drying hay.

PIT 1

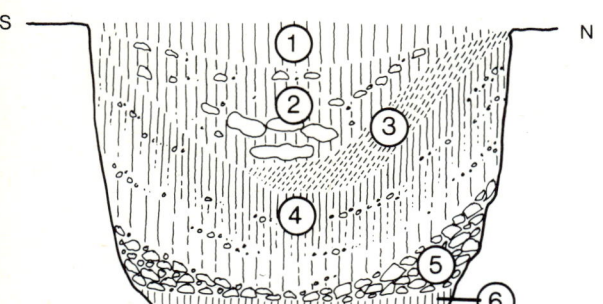

PIT 2

PIT 3

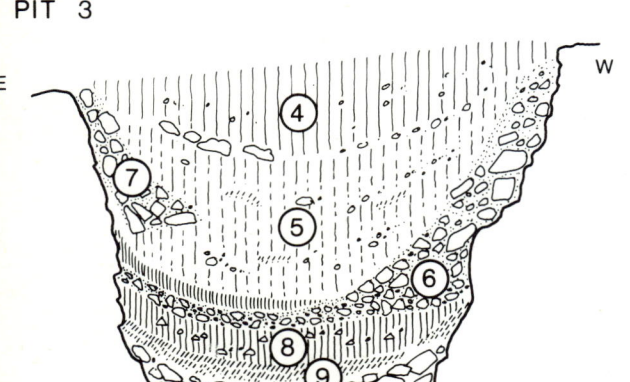

PIT 4

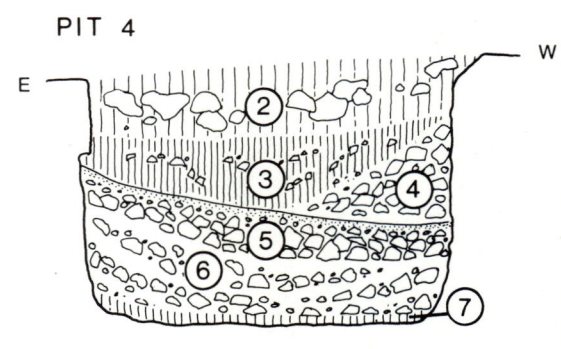

Fig.28 Pit sections from Chalton site 15

```
0                    1                    2 Metres
0    1    2    3                    6 Feet
```

Trackway

The excavated area was crossed by a trackway represented by a slight hollow terraced to a maximum depth of 9 in (0.23 m) on the uphill chalk. The surface of the chalk was worn and sealed by a reddish clayey soil; the track was later than pit 3 but is otherwise undated.

General considerations

The nature of the site is difficult to define on such slight evidence. Very few sherds can be found when the field is ploughed, but this may be due to the fact that Roman and later ploughing has scoured away surface deposits. When a trench for a gas pipe was cut through the area to the north of the excavation, some traces of Iron Age occupation were recovered. This might suggest that the 1959/64 excavation lay on the southern extremity of an Iron Age farmstead.

SMALL FINDS (Figs.29 and 30)

From site 50

1   Lower stone of a saddle quern: upper greensand. Pit 1, layer 4.

2   Lower stone of a saddle quern: upper greensand. Pit 5, layer 2.

3   Upper stone of a saddle quern: upper greensand. Pit 5, layer 2.

From site 15

4   Bronze ring made from a single strip of metal bent round with ends overlapping. Pit 1, layer 2.

5   Antler tine cut off main antler and showing signs of wear at the tip.
    Pit 3, layer 5.

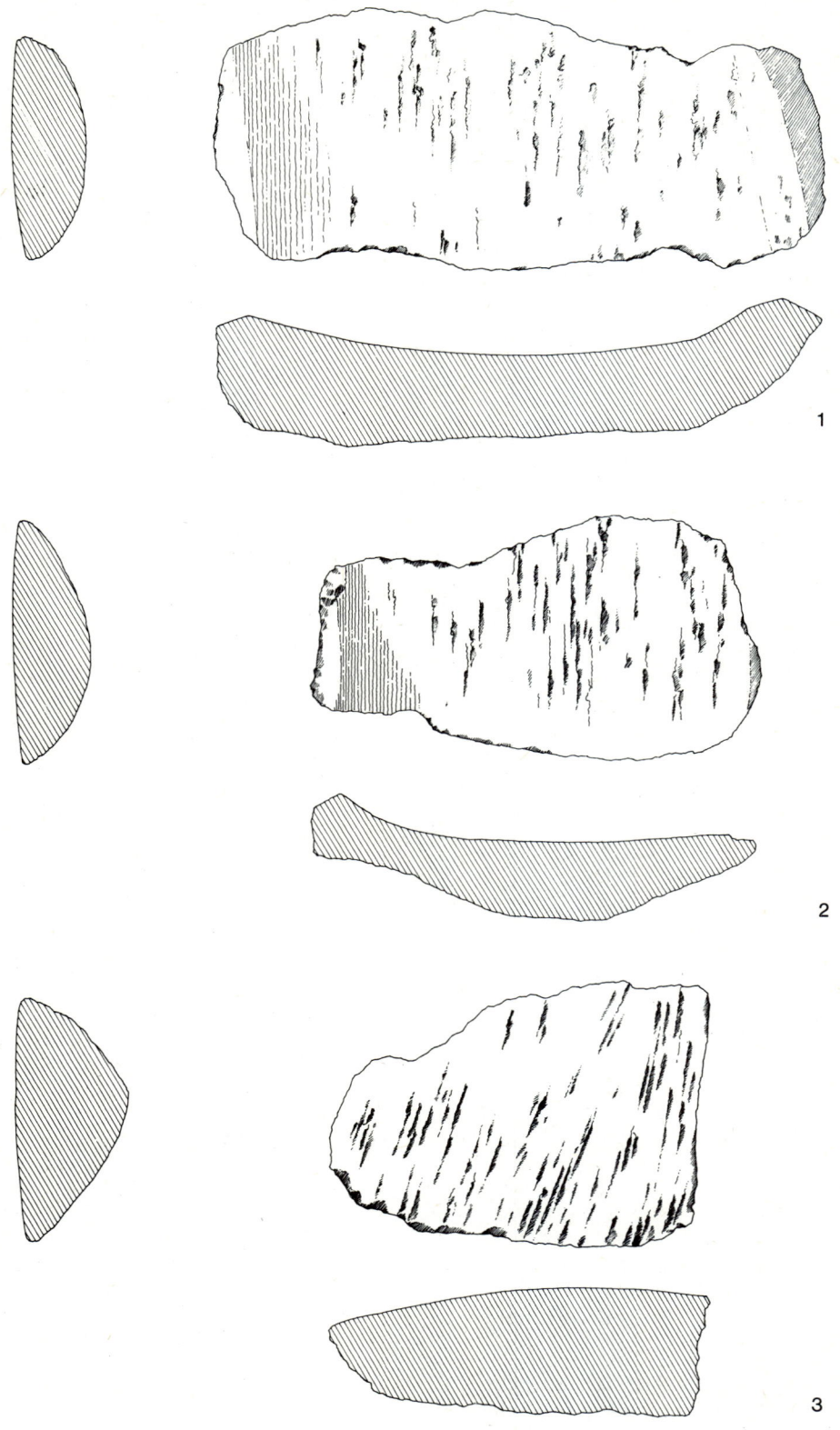

Fig.29 Querns: scale ¼. Site 50

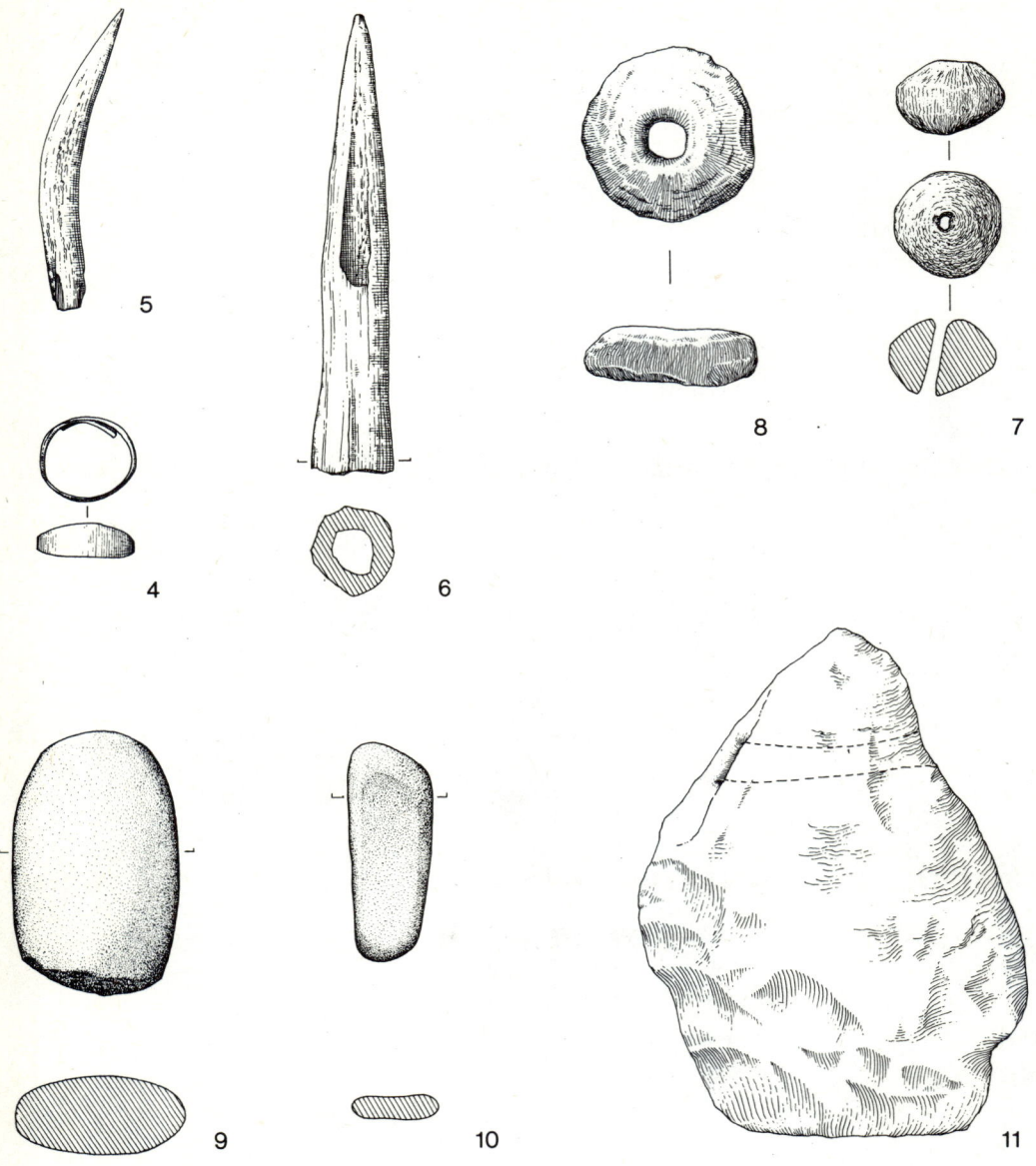

Fig.30   Small finds: scale ⅓. Site 15

6   Long bone cut to a point: shows signs of wear. The core has
     been removed, possibly for hafting.
     Pit 3, layer 5.

7   Pottery spindle whorl: grey-brown flint gritted fabric.
     Pit 4, layer 3.

8   Perforated chalk disc: roughly cut, possibly a spindle whorl.
     Pit 3, layer 4.

9   Pebble used as a rubbing stone
     Pit 3, layer 5.

10   Pebble used as a rubbing stone.
     Pit 1, layer 4.

11   Roughly cut triangular block of chalk perforated across the
     apex. Either a loom weight or a thatch weight.
     Pit 3, layer 1.

12, (Not illustrated) Two corroded strips of iron *c*. 1 cm wide:
13   possibly part of a binding (Now missing).
     Pit 3, layers 5 and 10

14   (Not illustrated) Corroded iron strip. (Now missing)
     Pit 1, layer 4.

THE POTTERY

The two sites have produced groups of pottery of differing
dates within the Iron Age, the finds from site 50 wholly pre-
dating those from site 15. The published sherds will be described briefly before the problems of dating are considered.
In the case of the earlier group from site 50, in which fabric
variations are considerable, a description of each sherd is
given. All the pottery from site 15, on the other hand, is
very similar in fabric and technique of manufacture, thus
allowing a more abbreviated descriptive treatment.

Site 50: Description of the illustrated sherds (Figs.31–33)

From Pit 1

1   Large thick-bodied storage jar (rim and base illustrated, body
     and shape uncertain). Hard black-brown ware with various-

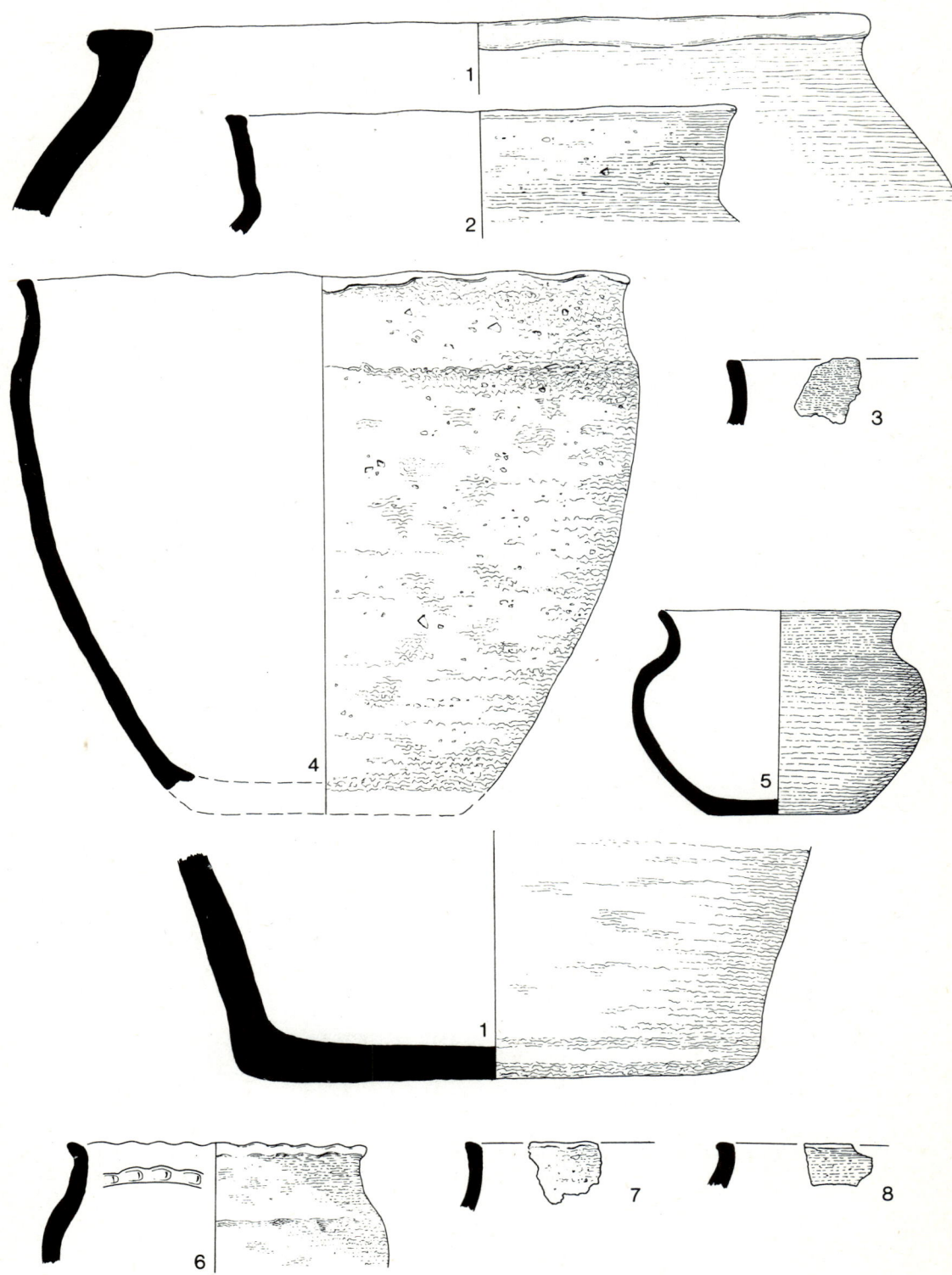

Fig.31   Pottery: scale ¹/₃. Site 50. Nos. 1–5 from pit 1; Nos. 6–8 from pit 2

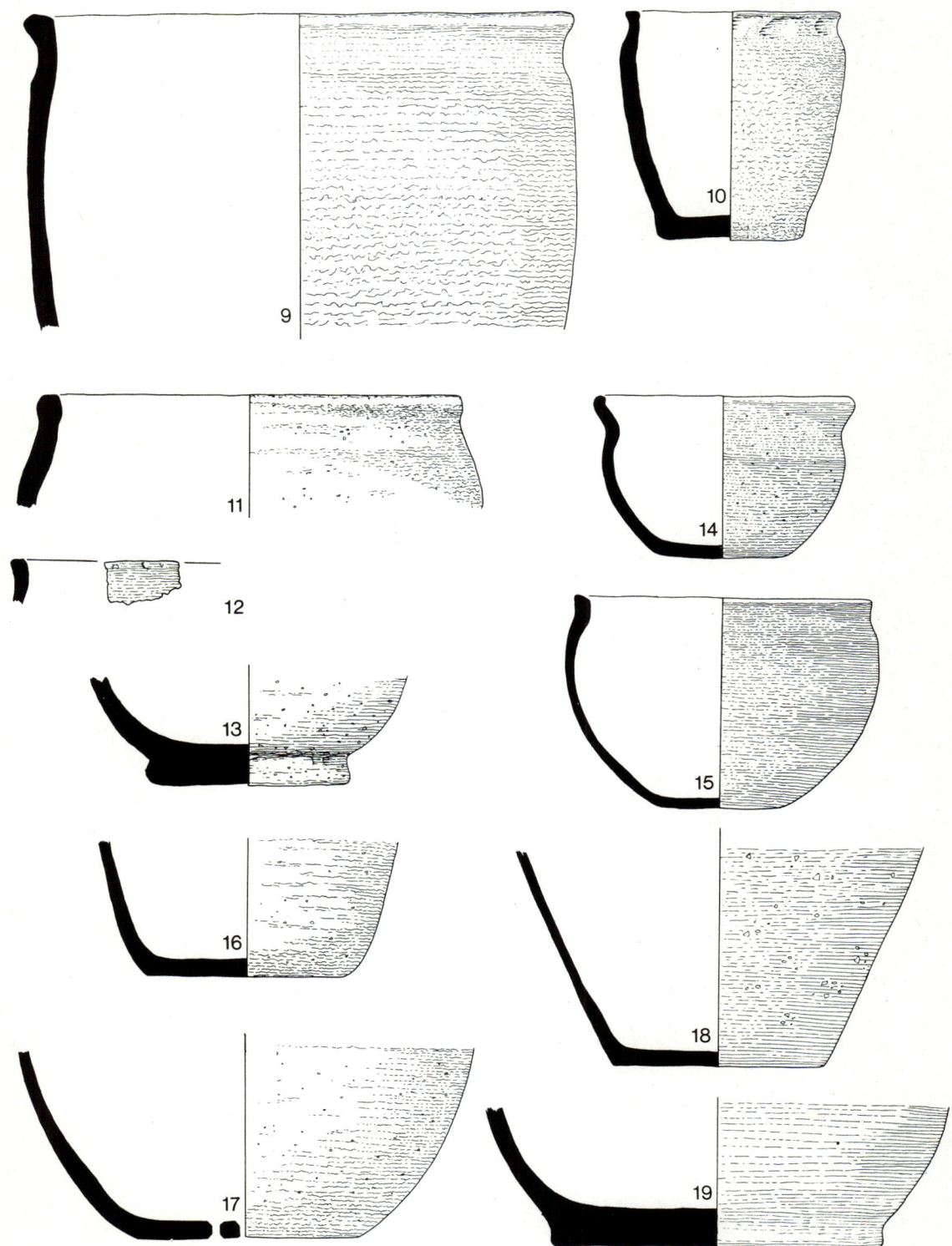

Fig.32   Pottery: scale $^1/_3$. Site 50. Nos. 9, 10 from pit 3; Nos. 11–19 from pit 5

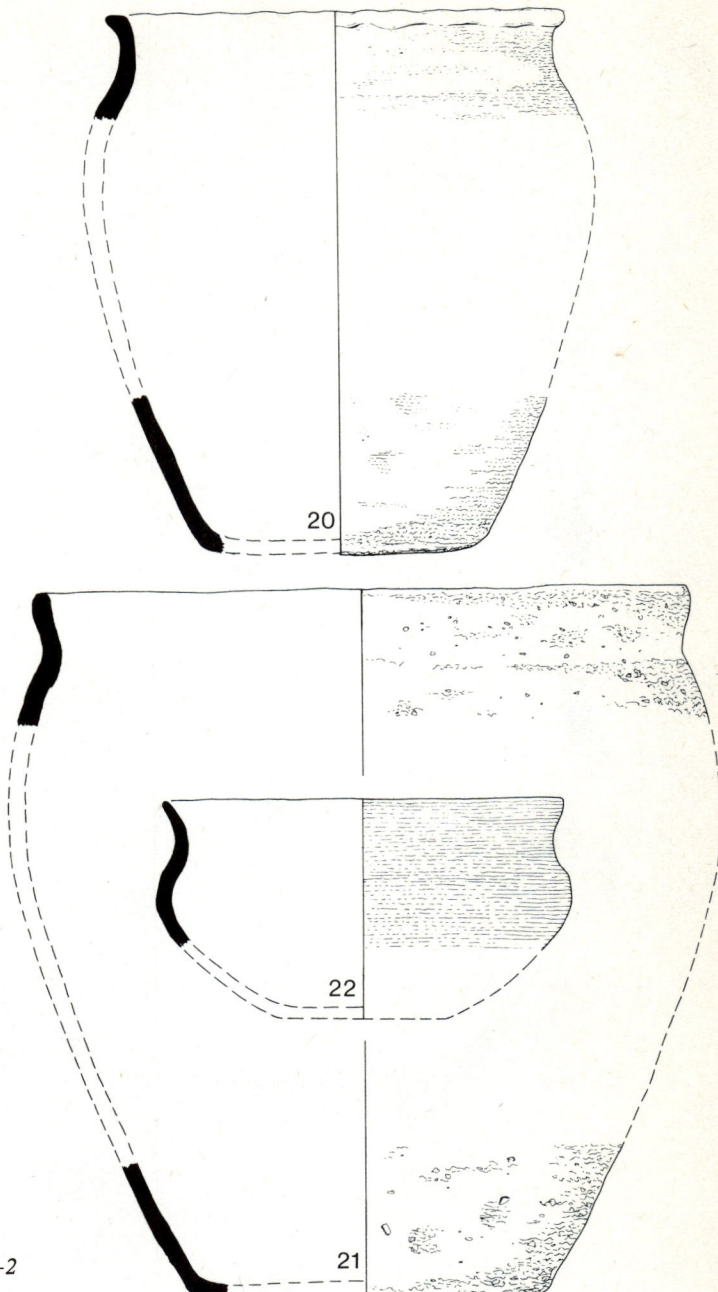

Fig.33   Pottery: scale ⅓. Site 50. No. 20 from pit 6; Nos. 21–2
from posthole 1

sized flint grits. Fired unevenly to a black-brown. Surfaces
smoothed but not burnished.
Pit 1, layers 2 and 4.

2   Jar: hard black ware with medium flint grit tempering. Fired
to ochre-brown on the surfaces. Surface smoothed, but not
burnished.
Pit 1, layer 2.

3   Jar: hard black ware with fine-medium flint grits. Fired black.
Surface smoothed, but not burnished.
Pit 1, layer 2.

4   Jar: coarse grey-brown ware with large flint grits. Surface
colour varies from black to red-brown.
Pit 1, layer 4.

5   Bowl: fine black ware with medium flint grits. Fired on both
surfaces to an ochre colour. The outer surface is lightly
burnished.
Pit 1, layer 4.

From Pit 2 (Fig.31, Nos. 6–8)

6   Jar: dark brown ware with medium-fine flint grits. Smoothed
surface fired black.
Pit 2, layer 1.

7   Jar: black sandy ware with medium-large flint grits. Fired
black and surface smoothed.
Pit 2, layer 1.

8   Jar: brown ware with medium flint grits. Fired black and
surface smoothed.
Pit 2, layer 1.

From Pit 3 (Fig.32, Nos. 9, 10)

9   Jar: hard grey sandy ware with medium flint grits. Fired
black-brown externally, smoothed but not burnished.
Pit 3, layer 3.

10   Jar: black ware with medium flint grits. Fired grey-black.
Smoothed but not burnished.
Pit 3, layer 3.

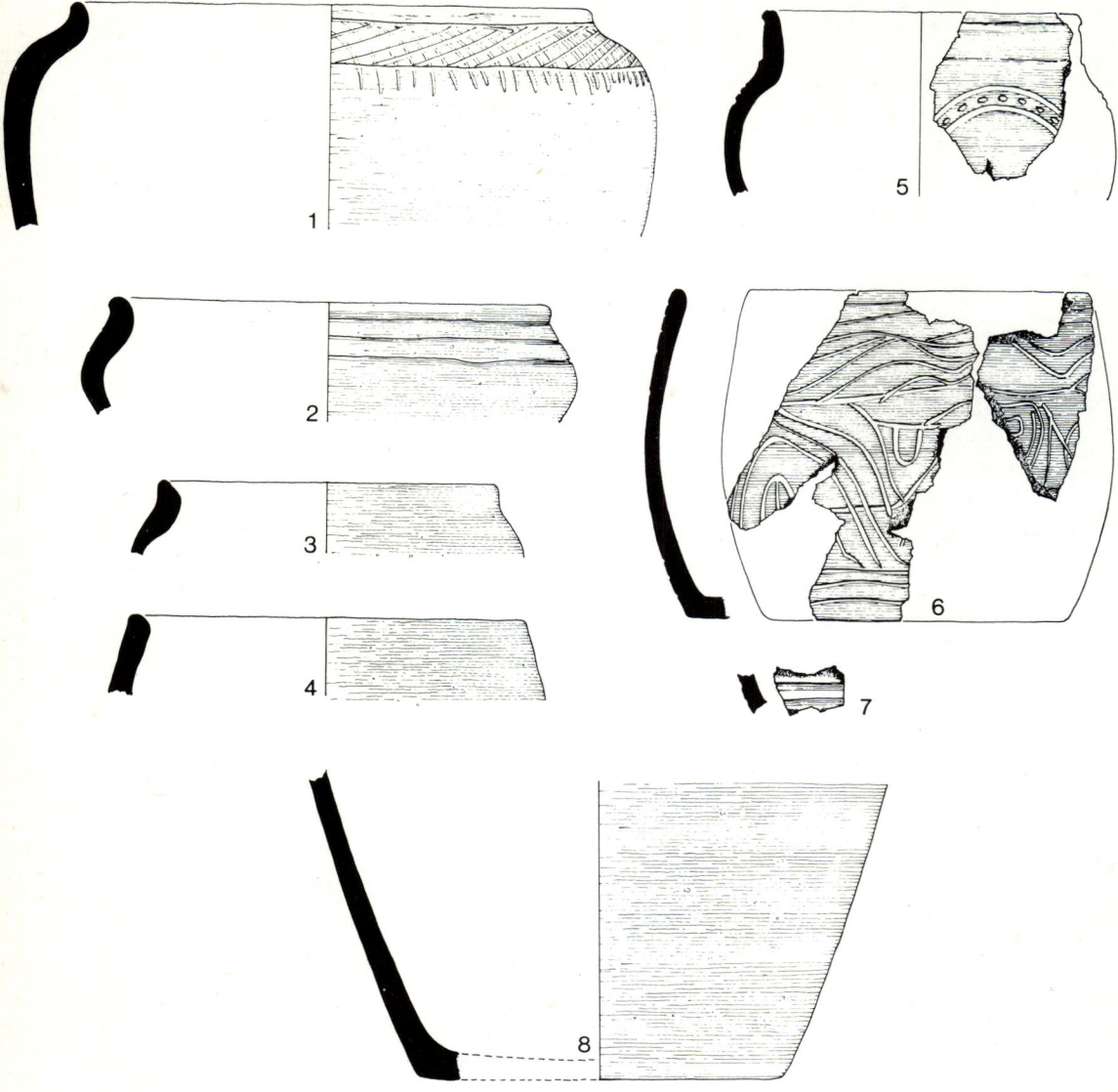

Fig.34   Pottery: scale ⅓. Site 15. Nos. 1–8 from pit 1

From Pit 5 (Fig.32, Nos. 11–19)

11   Jar: hard brown ware with medium and occasionally large flint grits. Fired grey-brown on the surface. Roughly smoothed;
Pit 5, layer 1.

12   Jar: black ware with medium–large flint grints. Burnished exterior.
Pit 5, layer 1.

13   Base: black ware with large flint grits. Fired to ochre-brown on the surfaces. Roughly smoothed but not burnished.
Pit 5, layer 1.

14   Bowl: grey-brown ware with fine flint grits. Fired black on the surfaces. Carefully smoothed and burnished inside and out.
Pit 5, layer 2.

15   Bowl: fine smooth grey-brown ware with occasional small–medium flint grits. Burnished inside and out.
Pit 5, layer 2.

16   Base: brown ware with medium flint grits. Surfaces smoothed and fired black.
Pit 5, layer 2.

17   Base with four perforations bored before firing: black-brown ware with medium flint grits. Externally fired to red-brown with the surfaces smoothed.
Pit 5, layer 2.

18   Base: black sandy ware with medium flint grits. Fired to ochre on the surfaces inside and out. Surfaces carefully smoothed.
Pit 5, layer 2.

19   Base: black sandy ware with medium flint grits. Fired to ochre on the surfaces. Carefully smoothed.
Pit 5, layer 2.

From Pit 6 (Fig.33, No. 20)

20   Jar: black sandy ware with medium flint grits. Fired black-brown. Surface smoothed.
Pit 6, layer 3.

From posthole 1 (Fig.33, Nos. 21, 22)

21   Jar: grey-brown ware with medium to large flint grits. Fired to an uneven grey-brown. Surface left rough.
Posthole 1.

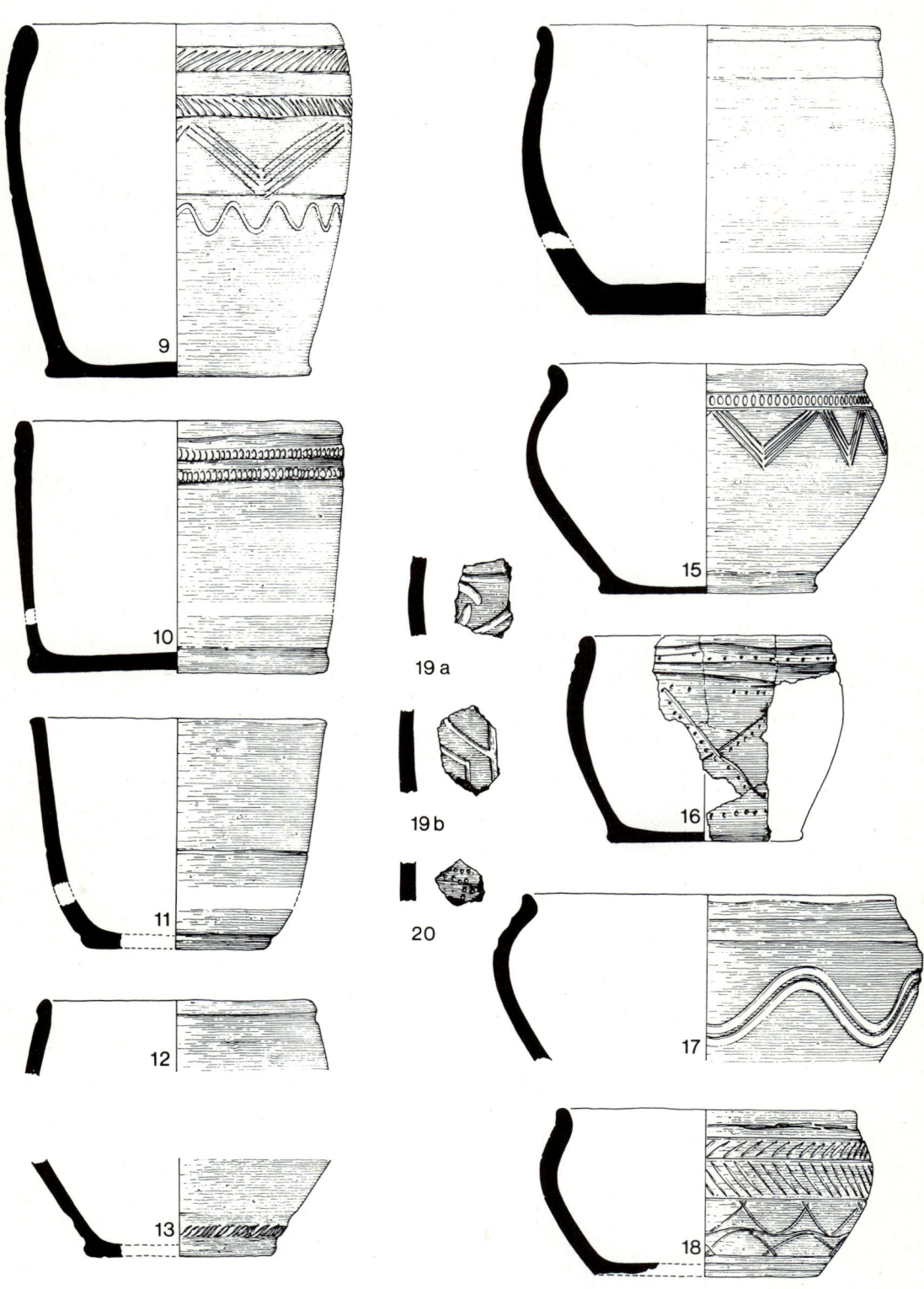

Fig.35   Pottery: scale ⅓. Site 15. Nos. 9–20 from pit 3

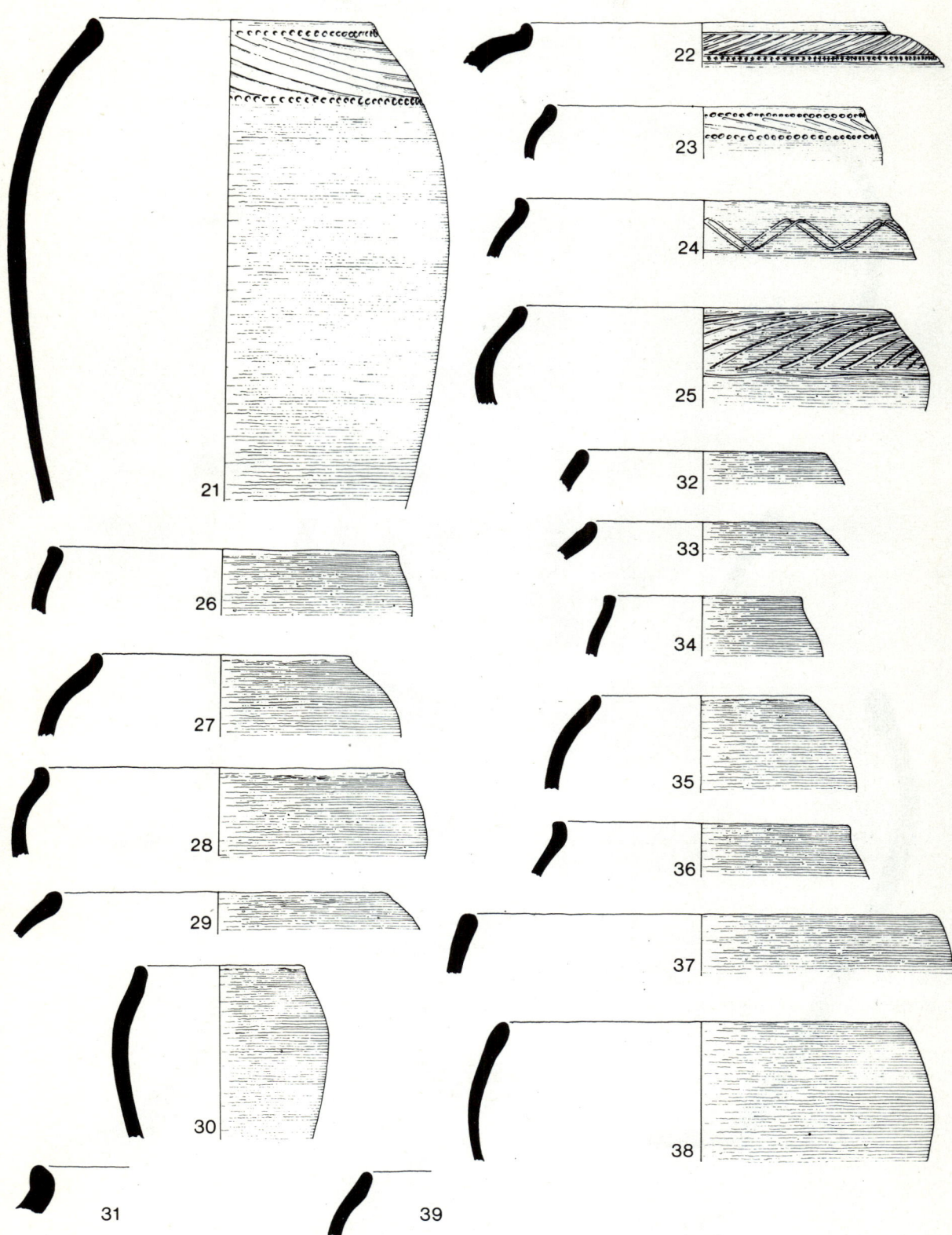

Fig.36   Pottery: scale ⅓. Site 15. Nos. 21–39 from pit 3 (continued)

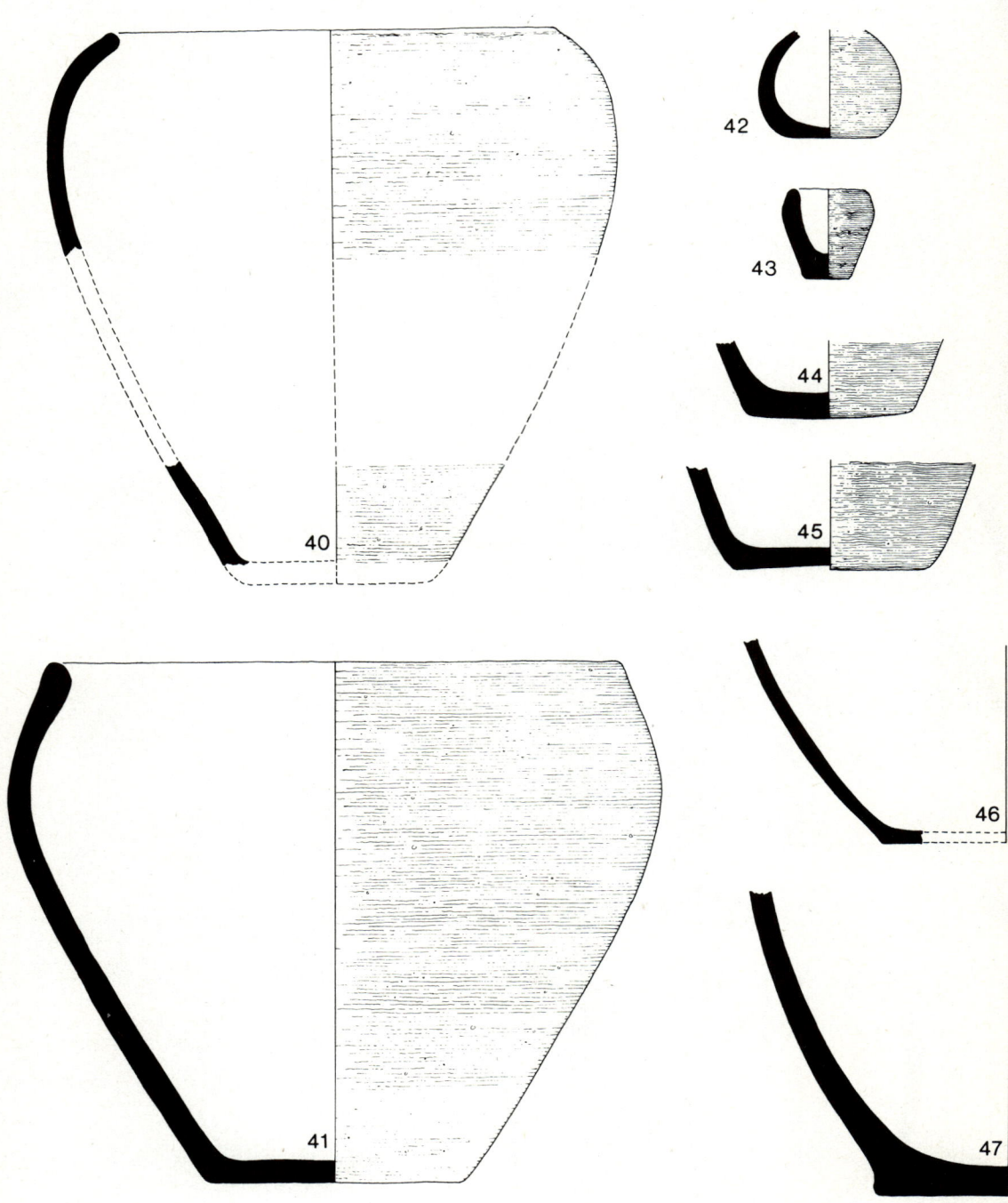

Fig.37   Pottery: scale ¹/₃. Site 15. Nos. 40–7 from pit 3 (continued)

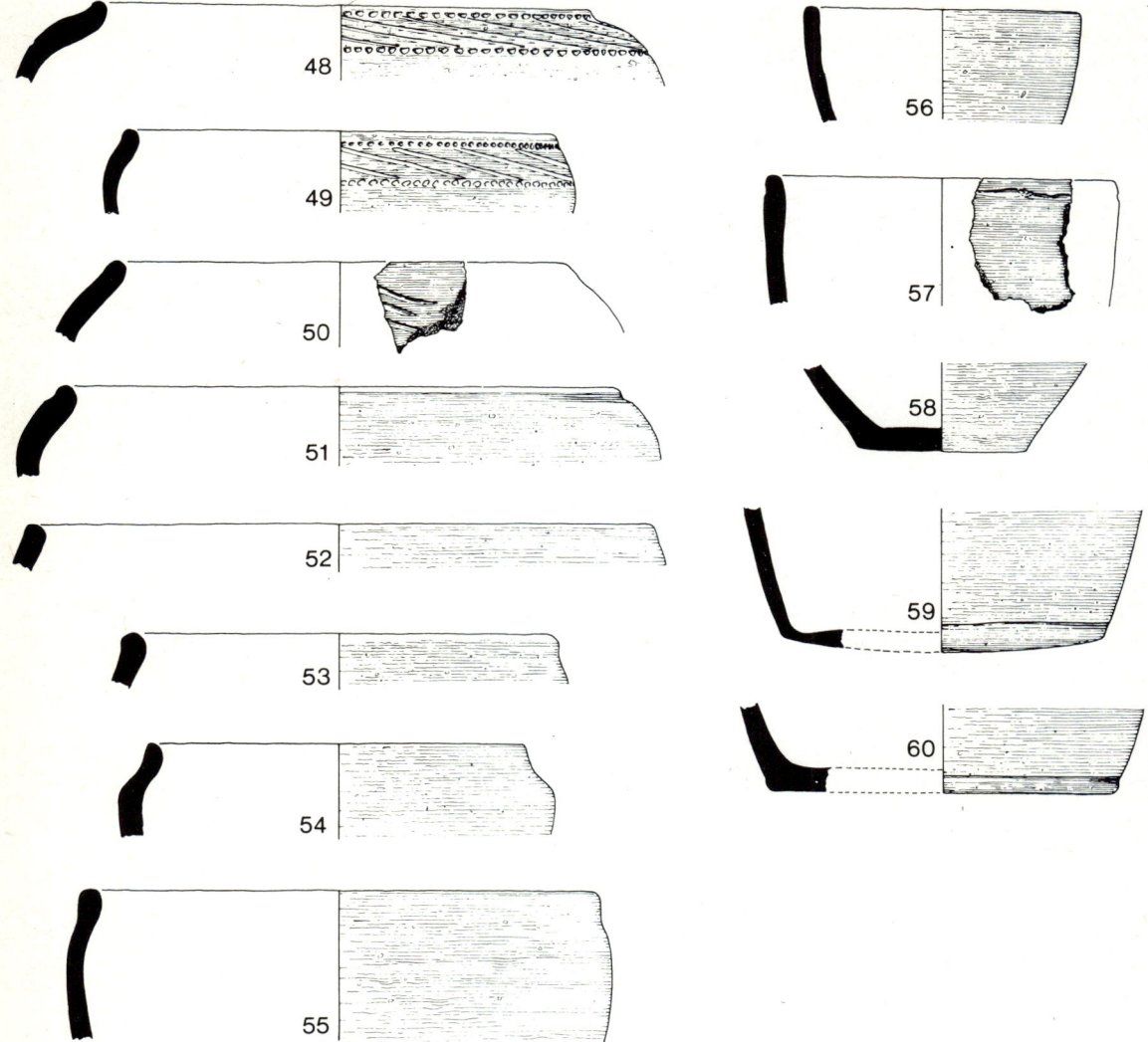

Fig.38   Pottery: scale ⅓. Site 15. Nos. 48–60 from pit 4

22   Bowl: fine grey-brown ware with medium flint grits. Fired
blackish-brown and carefully smoothed inside and out.
Posthole 1.

Site 15: Description of the illustrated sherds (Figs.34–38)

From Pit 1 (Fig.34, Nos. 1–8)

Nos. 1, 2, 4, 6, 7, and 8 were all made in even grey-brown fabrics
tempered with fine–medium crushed flint grits. The outer surfaces
were fired black in colour and were burnished. Nos. 3 and 5 were in
a fine grey sandy ware lacking the copious flint gritting. The surfaces were fired black. Decoration was shallow tooled when the pots
were leather-hard.

    layer 2: Nos. 1, 4, 8
    layer 3: No. 2
    layer 4: No. 3
    layer 5: Nos. 5, 7
    layer 6: No. 6

From Pit 3 (Figs.35–37, Nos. 9–47)

With the exception of Nos. 10, 12, 16, 19, 24, 34, 38, and 43, all
the illustrated pottery was made in an even grey-brown fabric tempered with fine–medium flint grits. Although the size and density
of the grit varies, a considerable similarity in fabric exists. Nos. 16,
19, 34, and 38 were made in a dark grey-black sandy ware without
grits. Nos. 10, 12, and 24 were also in a sandy fabric but with

occasional flint grits: No. 10 differed from the others in that it was
fired to an orange-brown colour. No. 43 was in a smooth grey-
brown ware without tempering.

For the most part (except No. 10) the vessels were fired grey or
black; the surfaces were always sealed by burnishing, the larger jars
exhibiting a more casual burnishing than the smaller jars and bowls,
which were usually finely finished. Decoration was always by means
of shallow tooling when the pots were in the leather-hard state.

Several of the more complete vessels were spread throughout the
pit in different layers, implying a degree of broad contemporaneity
in the filling.

    layer 3: No. 24
    layer 4: Nos. 20, 31, 36
    layer 5: Nos. 9–19, 21–3, 25, 28, 29, 32–4, 37, 39–43, 45,
        47.
    layer 6: Nos. 10, 14, 18, 21, 24, 40, 41, 44, 47
    layer 8: Nos. 9, 10, 11, 14, 18, 21, 26, 27, 32, 35, 40, 41, 44,
        46, 47
    layer 9: Nos. 9, 14, 30, 44
    layer 10: No. 12.

From Pit 4 (Fig.38, Nos. 48–60)

All vessels with the exception of No. 53 were made in an even fabric
tempered with fine–medium crushed flint grits. No. 53 was similar-
ly tempered but the matrix was sandy. All were fired to black, grey,
or grey-brown, except No. 54, which was in an oxidized fabric. Ex-

ternal surfaces were burnished and decoration was executed by means of shallow tooling when the fabric was leather-hard.

layer 3: Nos. 48–56 and No. 60
layer 6: Nos. 57–59.

DISCUSSION

Pottery from site 50

All the pottery from site 50 may reasonably be regarded as being broadly contemporary, since a similar range of types and fabrics occurs in each closed context. Three generalized types can be distinguished:

a. large storage jars: eg No. 1

b. jars in coarse wares, usually with slackly defined shoulders: eg Nos. 2–4, 6–12, 20, 21.

c. bowls in fine fabrics with burnished surfaces with outbent rims: eg Nos. 5, 14, 15, 22.

There remain a range of bases, most of which would belong to the jar type with the possible exception of No. 13, the form of which is uncertain. The fabrics are all flint-gritted to some degree and could all have been made in the vicinity.

The broad chronological development of pottery in south-east England is now well established and has been briefly discussed elsewhere (Cunliffe 1974a). In summary it may be said that before the development of saucepan pot types, in the middle of the pre-Roman Iron Age, two chronologically distinct assemblages can be recognised: 'Kimmeridge–Caburn style' and 'Park Brow–Caesar's Camp style'. The Kimmeridge–Caburn style is typified by sharply angled bipartite bowls, often decorated with cordons or stamped or incised decoration, tripartite jars with out-flared rims, and coarser jars usually with sharp shoulders decorated with slashing or finger impression (Cunliffe 1974a, figs. 3: 4, and A: 3). Locally this range of types is known from Stoke Clump, near Chichester (Cunliffe 1968), a rectangular enclosure on Portsdown near Portsmouth (Bradley 1969), and is represented among the early sherds from The Trundle (Curwen 1929, pls. X, XI). Exact dating is impossible, but must centre on the 6th century, probably extending into the 5th.

The second local style, the Park Brow–Caesar's Camp style, develops out of the first and probably spans the period from the 5th into the 3rd century. It is to this group that the Chalton site 50 assemblage belongs. Throughout the two centuries or so to which the style is assigned, there was, of course, change. It is possible to suggest, for example, progressive stages in the evolution of the coarse jar form from the sharply angled type of the Kimmeridge–Caburn style to the almost straight-sided versions such as Fig.32, No. 9, while the bowls can be arranged in a sequence from the bipartite angled types to simple forms similar to Fig.32, No. 15. Superimposed on these developments, external influences can be traced from the Thames valley and from northern France, and minor localized preferences of style appear. At present it must be admitted that these arguments are based largely on a subjective assessment of typology and, until more closed groups are available, should not be pressed too far. To illustrate the point, however, it could be argued that the range of types from pit 5 are 'more evolved' than those from the other pits.

In the general vicinity of Chalton, several assemblages of broadly similar type have been recorded, for example from the early phases of St Catherine's Hill (Hawkes, Myres, and Stevens 1930, figs.11, 12). Torberry (above, pp. 15–24), Wallington – Military Road site (Hughes 1974), and from the George Inn, Portsdown (Bradley and Lewis 1968). Some early sherds from The Trundle (Curwen 1929; 1931) are also in the same category. The wider distribution of the generalized Park Brow–Caesar's Camp style has recently been plotted (Cunliffe 1974a, fig 3: 4) and need not further concern us: extensive parallel quoting is of little value.

All the types present at Chalton can be found among contemporary assemblages further west in Wessex, where I have suggested the name 'All Cannings Cross–Meon Hill style' to contain the material. Similarities are indeed striking, the only significant difference being that in Wessex a specialized type of hematite-coated bowl, decorated with cordons and scratched decoration, commonly occurs. This type is likely to have been made in a localized production centre and distributed to a restricted market area. In other words, it could be said that the Chalton site 50 group belongs to a ceramic continuum which spanned southern Britain from the 5th to the 3rd century, within which minor regional and chronological differences are observable.

The transition from the early pre-Roman Iron Age pottery like that from Chalton site 50 to the characteristic smooth dark 'saucepan pot' types of the middle period is difficult to trace with precision, but the group from the in-filled cross ditch at Torberry provides a good range of what might be regarded as transitional types, followed by several different groups, all within the saucepan pot range, dating very approximately to the 3rd–2nd centuries BC. These matters are discussed in more detail above (pp. 23–4), where the broader context is considered.

Pottery from site 15

The pit groups from Chalton site 15 fall firmly within the saucepan pot range. A comparison of the illustrations will show that all three pits which produced pottery are likely to be broadly contemporary. Three basic types are represented:

a. jars incurving at the top

b. saucepan pots with vertical or slightly convex sides

c. bowls.

The fabrics are all well fired, usually flint-gritted, smoothed or burnished on the surface, and sometimes decorated with shallow tooling.

The different regional variations within the 'saucepan pot' continuum have been outlined elsewhere (Cunliffe 1974a, 42–4), and are referred to above (pp. 23–4). Chalton, like Torberry, falls within the distribution area of a local style which I have called the 'St Catherine's Hill–Worthy Down style', distributed widely over the territory between the Test valley and the river Arun. Within this area slight regional variations occur and, as would be expected, sites towards the periphery of the zone share characteristics with neighbouring areas.

Within a single style-zone one would expect to be able to trace differences between groups of different dates where sufficient material is available. This is at last becoming possible within the large collection of pottery from the hillfort of Danebury, Hants., but elsewhere in the region most assemblages known at present are too small for division. The groups from Torberry and Chalton site 15, however, present interesting contrasts. Since the sites are only 4 miles (6.4 km) apart, such differences as exist are more likely to be chronological than regional. The basic difference lies in the prevalence of the well made bowl type at Chalton, particularly in pit 3. Although bowls occur at Torberry, the Chalton examples tend to be more sophisticated, with tighly moulded foot-rings, upstanding necks, and a more varied range of decoration. All these characteristics appear as a regular component in the later Atrebatic pottery of the region which had developed by the middle of the 1st century BC (Cunliffe 1974a, 92, and fig.A: 28): in fact, it could be argued that the southern Atrebatic assemblage evolved out of the saucepan pot style with relatively little outside influence, the only significant innovation being the regular use of the potter's wheel.

These typological observations, therefore, strongly suggest that the pottery from Chalton site 15, while still within the St Catherine's Hill—Worthy Down style, is later than the groups from Torberry and might be regarded as transitional between a typical saucepan pot assemblage and the succeeding southern Atrebatic style. Dating is still a matter of guesswork, but some time in the late 2nd or the first half of the 1st century BC seems likely.

THE ANIMAL BONES

By Judi Startin

A total of 482 animal bones were recovered, 270 from site 50 and 212 from site 15. 342 of these were identified, and of the remainder 94 fragments belonged to the mixed shattered skulls of one ox and two horses from site 50, pit 2. The numbers were not sufficient to merit any analyses being undertaken, save to establish the relative quantities of the species present by counting each fragment, and determining the minimum number of animals of each species. These results are given below:

	No. of fragments	%	Min. no. of individuals	%
Site 15				
Ox	28	15	3	16
Pig	17	9	4	21
Sheep/goat	141	73	10	53
Frog	4	2	1	5
Bird	2	1	1	5
Site 50				
Ox	85	57	8	38
Pig	14	9	5	24
Sheep/goat	27	18	4	19
Horse	23	15	3	14
Red deer	1	0.6	1	4

It may be worthy of note that the emphasis changes from ox (site 50) to sheep/goat (site 15), but no real importance can be attached to this when dealing with so small a sample. For the same reason, information about the age and state of the animals and the butchery practices on these sites cannot be very meaningful. Suffice it to say that ten specimens from site 50 and twelve from site 15 were those of immature animals, while seven from site 50 and three from site 15 bore chop marks. In addition, one ox metacarpal with a mid-shaft growth from site 50, pit 2, provided the only instance of disease.

ORGANIC REMAINS
From Site 15

A small quantity of wasp galls were found in pit 1. Mr A Corney submitted them to R B Benson, MA, Senior Principal Scientific Officer of the Department of Entomology, British Museum (Natural History). In a reply dated 2 November 1959, Mr Benson writes that they "proved to be the galls of a gall-wasp, apparently a species of *Cynips*, possibly *C. agama* Hartiz. I have shown the specimens to Mr R D Eady . . . he has now compared the specimens with recent galls and thinks they agree exactly. These are the galls which produce the sexual generation, and are to be found in the summer and autumn on the underside of oak leaves. This and several other species of *Cynips* are widespread in Southern England today".

The discovery of the oak galls raises several interesting problems, not the least because Pliny writes of oak galls providing tannin for the tanning of leather (*Nat. Hist.*, xvi, 26). It remains a possibility, however, that the galls found their way into the filling of the pit in recent times by the agency of a burrowing animal.

ACKNOWLEDGMENTS

The two sites would not have been discovered and excavated had it not been for the interest and enthusiasm of the owner of the land, Mr John Budden. Mr A Corney of the Portsmouth City Museums readily placed his notes of his excavations at site 15 at my disposal and made the finds available to me, while Mrs Jo Chaplin took an active part in the examination of site 50. In addition to the above I would also like to record my thanks to Mr Mike Rouillard for drawing the pottery and finds from site 50.

The material from site 15 is on loan to Portsmouth City Museum. The finds from site 50 are stored by Mr Budden at Manor Farm, Chalton, Hampshire.

BIBLIOGRAPHY

Bradley, R, and Lewis, E, 1968 'Excavations at the George Inn, Portsdown' *Proc. Hampshire Fld. Club Archaeol. Soc.* **25** (1968), 27–50.

Bradley, R, 1969 'Excavations on Portsdown Hill, 1963–5' *ibid.* **24** (1967), 42–58.

Cunliffe, B W, 1966 'Stoke Clump, Hollingbury and the Early pre-Roman Iron Age in Sussex' *Sussex Archaeol. Collect.* **104** (1966), 109–20.

Cunliffe, B W, 1974a *Iron Age Communities in Britain* (London 1974).

Cunliffe, B W, 1974b 'Chalton, Hants: the Evolution of a Landscape' Antiq. J. **53** (1973), 173–90.

Curwen, E C, 1929 'Excavations in the Trundle, Goodwood, 1928'. *Sussex Archaeol. Collect.* **70** (1929), 33–85.

Curwen, E C, 1931 'Excavations in the Trundle' *ibid.* **72** (1931), 100–50.

Hawkes, C F C, Myres, J N L, and Stevens, C G, 1930 *St. Catherine's Hill, Winchester* (Winchester 1930).

Hughes, M, 1974 'M27 — South Coast Motorway — Rescue Excavations of an Iron Age site at Wallington Military Road, Fareham, 1972'. *Rescue Arch. in Hants.* 2 (1974), 31–96.

Plate I   General view of Torberry hill from the north (Photo: National Monuments Record)

Plate IIa   Torberry, Sussex: The inner entrance showing the cross-ditch terminals. View looking east

Plate IIb   Torberry, Sussex: East entrance, south ditch terminal, showing stone revetting wall in the ditch with chalk-block packing and outer face of gate wall

Plate IIIa   Torberry, Sussex: East entrance; posthole 10. View looking east with posthole half-excavated

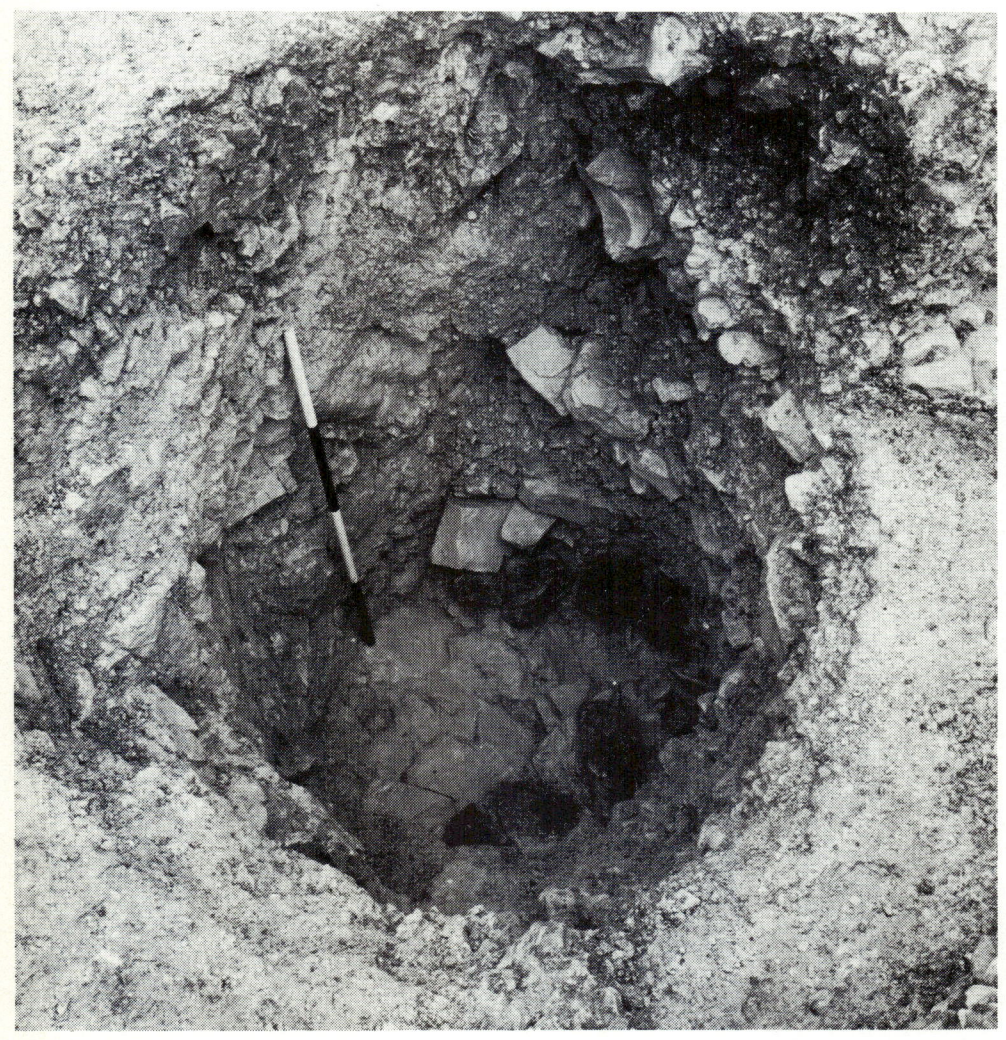

Plate IIIb   Torberry, Sussex: East entrance; posthole 9 with filling of post 'void' removal and packing still in position. The stone block on the bottom was used to level the post base

Plate IVa   Torberry, Sussex: East entrance; wall showing face and tumbled rubble half excavated in trench AI. View looking south

Plate IVb   Torberry, Sussex: East entrance; basal stones of wall on north side of entrance way in trenches BII, CII, BI, CI. View looking east

Plate Va   Torberry, Sussex: East entrance; wall face in trench AIV. View looking south

Plate Vb   Torberry, Sussex: East entrance: wall face in trench AIII. View looking south

Plate Vc   Torberry, Sussex: East entrance: wall face in trench AII. View looking south